Unfettered

A Philosophy of Education

James B. Barlow & Anil B. Naik

Copyright © 2016 James B. Barlow and Anil B. Naik

All rights reserved.

ISBN: 1539587355
ISBN-13: 978-1539587354

DEDICATION

This book is dedicated to our families, our students, and students everywhere.

CONTENTS

1	Introduction	7
2	Freedom	10
3	A Positive Mentality	11
4	Critical Thinking	14
5	Grades	20
6	Absence of Fear	24
7	Love	27
8	Creativity	28
9	Student Evaluation and Testing	32
10	Competition and Cooperation	35
11	Indoctrination	38
12	Self-knowledge	41
13	Personal Responsibility	44
14	Being a Good Student	47
15	Textbooks	49
16	Class Choice	54
17	Attendance	57
18	Extracurricular Activities	61

19	Individualized Learning	63
20	Syllabus	66
21	Everyday life	69
22	Content and Lasting Lessons	71
23	Electives	73
24	Unstructured Time	76
25	Self-discipline	79
26	Experiential Learning	82
27	Administration	87
28	Teacher Evaluation and Tenure	90
29	Teacher Collaborations	98
30	Culture	102
31	Preparing for the Workforce	105
32	Dropping Out	106
33	Community	109
34	Why Teach?	111
35	Conclusion: Purpose of Schools	113
	Acknowledgments	117
	About the Authors	118

INTRODUCTION

Students today are a different breed from those a generation ago and even more so than those a hundred years before. When the adults of today were young and sat in their classroom, they felt there was much to be desired in their schools and they wanted to make changes. So they made them. However, many of them have fallen into the same thinking as their parents—believing that their child's schools should be like theirs. Times have changed. The clientele is different and the nation's needs and desires are different. The children of today expect much better than what their parents had. It is time we gave it to them. We need to set a new course. Every one of us needs to begin to conceive of tomorrow's schools in a different fashion.

We are not academics or researchers, just two friends, a retired educator with over forty years of teaching experience and his former student. We are over fifty years apart in age and come from different family backgrounds, yet we both care deeply about education. Over the years, as we sat in restaurants over breakfast or in cafés over coffee, an inspired exchange occurred. We challenged each other on almost every aspect of our educational philosophy. We shared our personal experiences as a teacher and a student, and we reflected on what we liked and what could have been better. We inquired and listened, gave and took. We found so much to agree on. We found so much to be hopeful about.

Just because there are problems today in education doesn't mean that we're stuck. There is so much potential. We foresee a place where students not only acquire academic knowledge but also learn how to be in the world. It can be a positive fear-free environment in which young people can learn to thrive in changing times—where students are given the ability to seek out new challenges and create new experiences and be encouraged to do so. In this school, educators teach creativity and critical thinking, while cultivating self-discipline, self-knowledge, and freedom. Young people can leave this American institution open-minded and knowing the joys of cooperation, with a love of curiosity and learning, and aware of the world and their place in it. They can be unintimidated, unfettered and flexible in the years ahead. Our educational philosophy is that all students want to learn and can be taught.

This book is not an operational manual, full of research and detailed step-by-step guides. This is a philosophical look at what our schools are about, what they should be about, and the practical steps we can take to move it along. What drives our beliefs and structures our ideas about schools are our experiences in them. We thought about many of those big questions: What is an ideal society? What is possible? What can be taught? What is innate? What is the ultimate goal of an individual? Of a society? We found inspiration in the philosophies of many great minds before us, and we tried to place our understanding of their ideas within the context of the modern American school. We believe that to do fundamental change educators must examine their own motivations, ideals, and philosophy, as well as those of their school. Improving education will take more than finding little tricks for getting through the daily grind a little easier—it will require looking at what educators and students are grinding toward and why.

We do not believe that our book is anything more than a voice. Although suggestions for school reform should certainly

Introduction

come from many sources including educational researchers, parents, community members, administrators, teachers, and all students, both successful and struggling, there should be more emphasis on ideas coming from our teachers and students. They are the ones in the trenches. They know most clearly what goes on in the classroom and how school affects the lives of our young people.

As teachers talk to each other and to their students about what is going on in our schools, we would love more students to take it upon themselves to share their beliefs about what makes a good education and a positive educational environment. By interacting and sharing, we can learn together. We hope that in reading about our values and beliefs, you will think more about your own and take action where your heart leads you.

FREEDOM

Freedom is possible. Freedom is both being unencumbered from restrictions created by others as well as being able to control whatever you turn your efforts toward. It is the absence of possessiveness as well as the pursuit of new experiences with spontaneity and an emphasis on greater action.

A person of freedom does not become content or smug or stale. Resilient in novel situations, they are free from ruts that might develop due to past successes or failures. A person of freedom is unbound. And in this way, you could say that a free person is one with a great deal of control. They are the creator and master of their situations. They are highly aware and can immediately assess and act appropriately when others are incapable. A person of freedom is also one of great passion and concern, not only for oneself and others but also of the relationship between oneself and others.

We can teach that freedom comes, in part, from gaining self-knowledge through self-discipline and the pursuit of appropriate challenges. It also comes, in part, from letting go of societally-imposed restrictions, personally accepted and then self-imposed, such as discrimination, negative thinking and other kinds of mental limitations that hinder our actions. With these prisons then opened, we are released unfettered to take on life with freedom and enthusiasm.

A POSITIVE MENTALITY

People have the power to choose how to approach life, positively or negatively. We always attract into our lives whatever we think about the most. Our most common and our deepest thoughts along with the accompanying emotions, words, and actions create our reality. As we think, so shall we be; what we put forth, so shall we attract from the world.

We all use this power every day, many unaware that this process is constantly happening inside us. For example, in school, a new student worries about a certain class and the grades and examinations associated with it. He thinks the course will be difficult for him, and in fact, is creating a mental image of it being so. He also believes that the tests will be very difficult for him to pass. He does not choose to think about this class in terms of what he will learn and the topics covered—but rather in terms of the grades, and more specifically the negative aspects of grades. Now his mind is set. His mind is so wrapped around his presumed impending failure, he is not only distracted from seeing and acting on any positive possibilities that might arise, but his thinking also puts him in a state-of-mind that will hamper him from learning the material. He blocks himself from having a positive attitude and therefore the right learning mentality. In turn, the class is likely to be more difficult for him. He may learn less, and he may not do as well on the tests or in the class. He could have done otherwise. He could have formed a mental image from the start that the class is interesting and he will learn new and exciting things. It is amazing how a change of thinking improves his ability to enjoy the class and learn a great deal.

This process can be used anywhere, anytime, by anyone. Let's say after graduation a young woman enters the workforce and takes her first job. She has never done this type of work before. In fact, she has never done anything similar, yet she gives herself a chance. She doesn't make off-handed jokes and comments that she cannot do the job. She believes that despite her lack of expertise she could be good at her job and that it might help her. Her thoughts have effects; her words too. She believes her thoughts and words, and when minor setbacks occur (as they inevitably do), she sees them as the minor failures that always occur when one engages in new activities—as potential learning experiences in which something positive could be gained. She has an open mind. She is flexible and most probably happy. And in time, if she comes to feel that this job is not right for her and she is not succeeding and wants to find a new career, she will be better able to know what is right for her because she approached that first experience with a positive mentality and gained some self-knowledge. She has self-confidence; she has a willingness to try new things and challenge herself.

Thought, word, and action have real world consequences. When we have a thought, it must be exactly what we desire; when speaking of that thought, the words must be deliberate; and the actions that follow must reflect the thought. Moreover, certain positive thoughts are more productive than other positive thoughts. Instead of thinking 'I want to do' well in this class, the thought should be that 'I will do' well in class and 'I will learn' a great deal, for then we are doing something rather than wanting to do something. Now the individual is in control of their situation as the active force. When someone says "I will be excellent at such and such" they have a good perspective for future action.

A positive mentality

They set themselves up for success by having the right mindset.

Another technique used to achieving a positive mentality is the act of creative visualization, where you use your imagination to form a mental image of what you wish to create in life. You look into your ideal future and think about it as a reality—not merely as something that might happen. Holding that image in your mind and accentuating what is positive in the present helps you to create the thing you're thinking about. The key here is to change our thought process since many difficulties in life originate from blocks we have created for ourselves through negative thinking. Creative visualization is a method to prevent these blocks from arising.

A student convinced that thoughts are things having real world effects must also have the self-discipline to create the thoughts that they want in order to create the world they want for themselves. All successful people, irrespective of their endeavors, intuitively do so. They would do even better if they were consciously aware of this principle and focused on it to achieve results.

Teachers should understand this process, adopt it into their own lives, and encourage their students to practice it. The students will not only do better in class and be more willing to try something new, but it has the side effect of making them feel good about themselves. When students have a good self-image, it helps lead them to greater learning. This method will carry them beyond school and be a way to enhance all aspects of their lives.

CRITICAL THINKING

Learning to be a critical thinker isn't something you are forced to do for an exam and subsequently forget. Students can't "cram" for it like they can for a multiple-choice test. Young people are learning a mental process of actively and skillfully conceptualizing, evaluating, analyzing, synthesizing, and applying information to reach an answer or conclusion. They are learning a means to a way of seeing. It becomes part of their approach to being in the world, and this relationship with one's inquisitive nature stays with them long after graduation. If a student develops the skill of critical thinking, they become more enthusiastic about the world because new situations and facts don't intimidate them. They are less afraid of the unknown and more curious to engage in it knowing they have a means to try and understand the unknown.

Schools can teach the skills involved in thinking critically and see that it is practiced. The process begins by believing that everything must be evaluated. The student then determines whether or not the material intuitively makes sense. But, we can be easily fooled by our intuitions and the investigation must continue beyond our instinct. It must be put to the test of logic since logic is a component of critical thinking. One must ask, "Does the argument seem rational, based on the information I know? Is it consistent with other pieces of information I have?" Students should investigate the truth of the statements and the logical structure of the argument. Then the student must wonder about the motivations of the speaker, "Why are they telling me these things? What is their background and what are the known biases that could affect the information presented?" In this way, the student thinks about both the material and the source of the material. Good sources can have inaccurate material, and unreliable sources could have accurate material. After the student examines the causes and key factors of this information, they can be creative and assess it not only using the options presented, but also with new, previously unstated, options. Critical thinking is not simply a matter of logic or a process of elimination. The thinker must decide if the solution may exist beyond the offerings of others. Creativity is just as an important facet of critical thinking as logic.

Students can then go on to also examine how this new information could be used. Is it useful and what might be the possible results of its application? Where within their cognitive map does this fit? How can this piece work together with something already known to create a new concept? Which previously held ideas are now worthy of inspection because they and this new piece appear at odds? The teaching of critical thinking skills, required to achieve self-knowledge and to creatively build upon previous notions is a beautifully time-consuming process. So much growth occurs due to critical thinking.

Despite these positives aspects it appears that many young Americans are failing to develop this skill. University professors and employers find even the 'best and the brightest' struggle to think for themselves. Far too often they will ask questions like "what should I do?" or "what is the right answer?" and when academics and employers turn these queries back upon their questioners, these young people are confused, freeze up, and are unable to continue. Schools today are turning out many young people who are simply awaiting instruction on what to do and what to think.

Why is this occurring? Why are our young people like this? Why are young people graduating high school with an ability to restate 'the right answer' and a profound inability to engage in a process by which they themselves create solutions? One reason is that critical thinking has been pushed aside in school.

Some educators are recommending standardized testing because of the high standardized test results of schools overseas. When our media catches word of their test scores, there is rarely an inquiry of why these students are testing so much higher. It's not a news story that many of their schools focus on memorization, and these same students are not taught to analyze. American students are cast as slower academically compared to the rest of the world because of these test results. Pundits urge that we need more testing and more rigor so we can 'catch up' with the rest of the world. But do we really want to copy those educational systems? We Americans must ask ourselves an identity question, do we want the education of our young people to be judged principally by their ability to state facts or should they be judged on their ability to use facts? If we desire rote memorization, we can have our test scores go up and our boys' and girls' records will equal or exceed those of anyone in the world, of that there is no doubt. What makes American schools great is not its excellence in regurgitation, but its ability to produce students who will create when they are adults. Our youths can lead the world in creative thinking and ingenuity, but it seems that this goal is not quantifiable and cannot be summed into a tight news clip or sensational factoid. The real scandal is not that American schools have low test scores, the scandal is that American education is trading away one of its greatest attributes for one that is quantifiable, but meaningless.

Beyond this mimicry of other systems, critical thinking is also absent because there are educators who feel it cannot be taught to young people. A common criticism is that students, being young and new to the world, have neither the experience to put material in context nor the cognitive capacity to assess complex issues. But very few adult possess enough experience and background information to thoroughly consider multiple sides to an issue, and none of us are experts about everything. Simply because one is not an expert does not mean they cannot use their mind to evaluate matters. Adults think critically about ideas, be it the news or nutrition, based on what they know. And what they know comes from their background in life. Young people have less experience, but they do have some and can draw upon that experience when thinking critically. Since the act of regularly thinking critically will increase the cognitive abilities of the young person, it is important for adults to share their experiences and thoughts and to assist young people in becoming better in this process and to encourage it no matter the result or the limits of the intellectual rigor used. Young people make critical decisions every day: who to trust, how to act with others, and so on. Why would we not expect them to be able to think about and understand academic subjects or philosophies? Critical thinking is about being active in your actions, in your life, and in the world. So you see, critical thinking can occur at all ages.

Despite the benefits, some teachers do not like to have students take issue with what or how they teach and some instructors are extremely fascistic in not allowing students to voice their opinion. This does little good, although the teacher might be pleased since it creates strict order and gives them the sense of being respected. The reality is the teacher is not loved but feared, not respected but suffered through.

We should never forbid other people from trying, because in not trying they abrogate responsibility and leave all their thinking to others. This final point, on the deferring of critical thought, is worth a closer inspection. People cede their opinion, voice, and power to others for two principle reasons. One, an individual can believe that others have better information or are more experienced than they, therefore the individual trusts the other to make a good decision on their behalf. The second manifestation of this outsourcing of critical thinking comes from the knowledge that holding a contrary position will lead to displeasure from or expulsion from the group. Neither of these reasons are necessarily bad, and to be a functioning member of society it becomes helpful to occasionally engage in both. However, what remains vital is thinking; think about why you are relinquishing your opinion to someone else. It is wonderful to notice that even when we choose not to make a certain decision, we are still being a critical thinker by choosing when and to whom we cede our opinion. Simply being conscious of your motivations compels smarter decisions.

It is more than the individual who benefits from becoming a creative and analytical thinker. A democracy society also needs critical thinkers, for it is only then that the governance of the state becomes a conversation and the checks and balances between representatives and the represented is alive. Such people will shape public discourse and will examine and critique both the opposition as well as those who agree with them.

Additionally, the educational process improves from a classroom full of young people who think critically. When students do so, they engage the course material in a deep and personal way and by being involved in the subject, they are truly learning by taking an active role in their classroom. In this way, critical thinking leads to lively discussions, and when some students are vocal in their thoughts, it motivates others to be engaged and to share their opinions as well. A great classroom is one where students learn from each other. Great teachers realize that everyone benefits when any of us becomes a critical thinker.

Encouraging young people to think critically and actively is a sign of respect from the teacher. This respect further empowers the student in class and in life beyond school.

GRADES

Real learning flows from the natural desire to be curious, to explore, and to seek new experiences. Grades distract from the path to real learning.

We Americans are hung up on grades. Almost every student broods about the grade they are getting or the one they want. Too many teachers are stressed out over grades and progress reports. And the sweeping majority of parents confuse the letter grade with an indication of their child's intelligence, mastery of the content, proficiency with skill, or even with hard work. Our news reporters and politicians don't dream of criticizing the grading system because they fear being perceived as having soft standards. But grades, in fact, cause great harm and have no place in schools. We ought to get rid of grades.

Ideally, grades serve as an accurate representation of a student's learning—a form of measurement showing whether or not the student understands what the teacher is trying to teach. Schools want grades to be a condensed form of useful information which then allows students to know how they are doing and keeps the parents abreast on their child's progress. It then helps future teachers find appropriate places for further learning and assists colleges with admissions. This one-letter abbreviation for the young person's progress, however, is devoid of such useful information and it's deceptive in the message it conveys.

If the sole piece of communication from the teacher is the grade, then a grade's meaning ought to be very clear. If the feedback is a simple letter, then who ever reads that letter should have no doubt as to what it means. Stop lights have only three colors, but it is apparent to everyone what those colors mean. The symbolic meaning of a single-letter grade is very uncertain and inconsistent. Every teacher has their own idea of what an A is supposed to mean and what A-quality looks like.

Assigning grades isn't an objective task for the teacher, and the letters students receive don't have definitive meaning. Grades are subjective. Whether As are given in classrooms across the hall or across the country, young people receive identical letter grades for different levels of work, different levels of content knowledge, and different levels of skill proficiency.

The two major parties that see grades—parents and future educators—have no way to determine what level of learning was tied to the letter given. There is no sure-fire method to distinguish an easy grading teacher from a rigorous one; they have no way of knowing the student's growth or understanding by glancing at this one-letter abbreviation. How can students, educators, and parents respond to the child's needs when they don't even know what they are? The problem is not that there are exams and that there is feedback; the problem is the teacher casts a short symbol for a long series of events. There is no common understanding and no dialogue.

In addition to the problem of what grades are supposed to mean and how they're to be used, there is the problem with what grades do to children and the education system. Grades are wreaking havoc on young people's desire to learn. In a graded environment, students see their primary goal as the accumulation of those letters that are supposed to represent knowledge. They believe they're at school for the grade. And rather than have a growth mentality, they cling to the label of wanting to be an A student believing that success is defined by possessing these symbols. They likely hear ideas about the long-term importance of their grades: what they mean for college admissions, what college admissions mean for career prospects, and how their job will dictate their lifelong happiness. Many students become scared to experiment and would rather take easier classes and be guaranteed a good grade than explore and risk failure. Concerns over GPA reduce their motivation for unique challenges and the pursuit of self-knowledge. Moreover, intentionally or not, grades are a vehicle to create competition within students at the expense of knowledge. We cannot afford to overlook such psychological effects of a system where fear and pride become the student's primary motivators.

Knowing that grading is subjective doesn't have to be a problem. Rather than struggling to make grades more objective through uniform rubrics or increased standardization, we would be better off having assessments that admit to being subjective.

There are several alternative options to the grading system. One is a student portfolio. Portfolios can either highlight the student's best work or track all their labors so the student can reflect and learn from their past successes and failures. In both arrangements, students learn during the process of building their portfolio. Portfolios are also more understandable for outsiders (such as admissions counselors, future employers, and parents) who do not know the individual teacher like the student does.

Another possibility is a proficiency-based assessment. In this model, the teacher charts the student's progress towards a certain skill or knowledge goal. The academic content is a vehicle for teaching those skills. In this particular model, the student would potentially receive marks for specific skills, not just the one letter that summarizes all skills. In this system, a student can work on areas in which they need more time and are not punished for learning something a week after the rest of the class. The student is rewarded for learning, regardless of when they do so.

Both of these arrangements should be accompanied by a narrative assessment from the teacher. It would allow greater clarity in feedback for everyone involved. Whether by discussion or in writing, evaluation of the student's progress should not only focus on whether the material was understood and skills were mastered, but what the teacher recommends for further exploration. It's not enough to record what the student has or has not done; there must be a forward-facing view of where the young person can go.

These assessment methods encourage real work in school—projects, community service, internships and extracurricular activities, art, audio/video and essays. This process naturally leads to more lessons being individualized to meet the variety of needs for the variety of students. Differentiating instruction is easy when the student's goal is mastery of skills and ideas, and the content serves as a vehicle to get the students there.

Grades have behaviorally battered students and punished those who need to learn the material in different ways or wish to study new subjects. They are an inaccurate indicator of learning and ability. If there were no grades, all students, without fear, would be encouraged to engage in classes and explore new subjects simply to learn new things. A school without grades would emphasize developing competence in academic areas, more individualized learning, and more meaningful student assessment. Think of how this would positively affect their future lives.

School can be a place where we nurture childlike curiosity: where every day is a new experience, full of exploration and growth.

ABSENCE OF FEAR

Fear is a common and powerful emotion capable of affecting a person's every action and their worldview. This stifling emotion paralyzes one from taking positive action. There is an enormous difference between the helpful and useful moments of being concerned (an awareness of potentially negative events), as opposed to having fear which causes you to retreat from experiences in general. Fear causes people to take action—but it is reactive, not proactive.

Humans, young and old, male and female, all over the world share many similar common fears. Many fear that their lives have no purpose. They fear that regardless of the choices they make, they may not succeed. This is another way of saying that nothing they do makes any appreciable difference in important matters. They fear defeat, shame, rejection, and loneliness. They fear that they do not have freedom from a future determined by forces beyond their control. The fears that people share around the world are countless.

At some point during the early years of education, students learn that fear is a key driver in the classroom. Many schools use fear as a tool to motivate "success." The exploitation of fears stifles, intimidates, and manipulates students. Young people learn that they must complete assignments, not for the knowledge they acquire or because they want to, but because of fear of a bad grade

Absence of fear

or reprimand from the teachers. By fearing failure, many become apathetic to class, the material, and school at large. Apathy shields them from the emotional effects of failing, because if they don't try and don't take up the challenge themselves, they won't view failures as their own. But apathy is not the only response to not being deemed a success. Others respond to this stress by only engaging in that which they think they will succeed. They don't experiment, take risks, or try new things. It is disheartening to know that students reject experiences because of fear, and yet, many young people determine the course of their life in just that way. Eventually, by beginning to fear any change, they start to withdraw into themselves and see the outside world as threatening. Not only do new activities threaten them, but also new ideas and new information. Under these conditions, critical thinking does not exist; creativity is lost; and curiosity is muted.

Fear should not be a primary motivating factor in one's life. It should not dictate the life we lead.

Most fears originate from the belief of the limits of one's own power. Specific fears are a particular manifestation of a general feeling that there is much beyond one's understanding and control. But we all have much more control over our lives than we believe.

Schools should make an active effort to increase students' knowledge, as well as demonstrate through action the tremendous amount of control one can have over one's life. Through knowledge, the student gains greater understanding about the world and relationships within the world. This potentially reduces a student's general fear of things unknown. Additionally, by learning that they have control of their life, the student realizes their power to produce desired effects, which may compel them to enter into situations where previously fear would have prevented it. They take on an attitude of seeking action and involvement.

Administrators can make certain policy adjustments to increase the power young people have to produce the changes they might desire in their life. A few examples could be to eliminate grades and standardized tests, create unstructured time, and allow students to choose their classes. If schools take these steps, fear will be far less likely a primary motivating factor that directs student's decisions in both their academic life and home life. As opportunities increase for students to shape their destiny, hopefully, those young people will see new experiences as opportunities that can benefit rather than harm them. Their motivation will become increasingly intrinsic.

There is no reason our lives should be dictated by fear.

LOVE

Love is the strongest philosophical foundation. To love is to know the object of your feeling as an extension of yourself. Indeed to love others is to see them not as someone who brings you happiness or whom you like being around or whom you depend upon, but as a continuation of you. It is possible to have this feeling of love to all people, all places, all creatures, and all things.

Teachers have the opportunity to see their students as connected to themselves and show them that they and their peers are linked to each other.

CREATIVITY

The benefits of creative thinking exist in all pursuits, from history to mathematics, and from physical education to literature. It serves more than artists and musicians—it can improve the thinking of all individuals by challenging the mind to see different relationships. The imaginative mind is an open mind, assessing what they see in the outside world and exploring unstated options by formulating new ones. These qualities are an essential component not only to critical thinking but also to actively participate in one's life. There are no limits to the application of creative action and thought.

Teachers can ensure that there is a climate in the classroom where creativity can flourish. A friend of Jim Barlow told him a sad story about how she became convinced never to try to be creative. It was the fall of her third-grade year. Her teacher announced that the class would draw Halloween pictures and that they would begin by drawing pictures of a black cat on a fence. She imagined what the cat looked like and used the image in her mind's eye, drew a cat and was very proud of the result. When the teacher looked at her picture, he said it would not suffice and told her to try again. So again she drew a cat on a fence and showed it to the teacher. The teacher once more stated that it was unacceptable and told her to try again. He obviously had an image in mind as to what he wanted. The girl tried again, yet still did not meet the demands of the teacher.

According to the woman, he then drew a picture of a cat on a fence, handed it to her and said, "Now take this picture and draw a cat on a fence the right way." She took the teacher's vision of a cat on a fence and copied it onto her paper—and at last, had done the assignment correctly. What the teacher wanted was two circles, one on top of the other, with the bottom one touching the top of the fence. He wanted the tail hanging down from the bottom loop and two ears perched on the top. Whiskers, eyes, nose, and mouth were needed to be added to the top circle. According to the teacher, only then was there a cat.

The woman telling the story explained to Jim that this one event killed her creativity. She wanted to be a good student and make her teacher happy, and as we have seen, this instructor bestowed praise on pupils who always conformed without deviations. The girl felt, from then on, in order to be a good student she must always follow orders to the letter. She ceased taking the initiative and exploring; she stopped being creative. Many students, especially in the early grades take to heart everything they are told, which often is then indelibly etched in their minds. That event stayed with her onto college.

Now, her teacher is likely to have a different recollection of those events, and the story as explained by his student may not be wholly accurate. But what the girl perceived was the truth to her, and we must realize that perception is everything when it comes to teaching.

What happened in that anecdote ought not to have happened. Teachers are in the education business and creativity is a vital part of education; eliminating creativity eliminates a necessary part of education. Its place in formal education furthers the concept that the world is not simplistic and it cannot be understood through rote memorization, that answers don't live in a book somewhere, only needing to be found. Schools have a duty to teach that thinking outside the box could lead to finding novel solutions to problems and that schooling is not only about understanding what came before, but also looking forward.

Teachers have an important job ahead of them. Creativity in the classroom must be a goal every day. Teachers must actively encourage it through student choice and the creation of an environment where the student is not afraid. Students can be shown that through creative expression they may be better able to express their feelings and comprehend issues of inner tension. Students should know that being creative is a good thing and highly desirable and the more it is practiced, the easier it gets.

While creativity is hard to teach through traditional instruction and lectures, it is possible to make it a part of the school experience. Creativity can be fostered by providing students choice—be it through electives, assessments, or unstructured time—and through authentic experiential learning.

Another way adults can show young people how creativity can blossom within themselves is by urging students to quiet their active thoughts from time to time and allow their subconscious to direct the thought process. In this way, the student is shown that calming the mind can net new ideas.

In our modern world, it has become commonplace to spend all our time doing something. Whether that something is chatting on the cell phone or constantly rechecking our email or flipping channels during commercial breaks, we seem always to find distractions to fill our time. With the mind continually occupied in this way, we rarely take a break and assess what we are doing and what we have done. And rarer still, do we budget time to do nothing at all. In the stories of Sherlock Holmes, that famous fictional detective would take a respite from his investigation and play his violin. Often while performing a piece for himself in his quiet study, he would come upon some bit of information he had previously overlooked. This is no literary ruse to excite the reader, but rather a reality of how our mind works. Acts such as a long walk can result in new ideas. It is joked that some of the greatest innovations were arrived at while in the shower or just as someone was crawling into bed. This is no surprise. Our conscious mind tends to keep us tuned to preexisting patterns of thinking and options already presented.

True creativity arises when people have self-confidence and freedom of thought.

STUDENT EVALUATION AND TESTING

Every act that occurs in a school can be educational and forward looking. Even assessing the student can be an experience where the student learns through the process of taking the test. By providing new and challenging experiences as opportunities for assessment, teachers can force higher order thought and receive more accurate feedback. This type of evaluation is possible and can be done in a way that causes the student to enjoy evaluation because it is a way to share their understanding and learn deeper. Every act can help the student go further.

There are two major types of evaluation: one tests the recollection of factual information and the other tests for conclusions using factual knowledge along with interpretation. Using recall testing as the only evaluative tool is the lazy way out of the challenging and time-consuming process of student evaluation. It is a fast way to get a grade for the students, but it only measures a young person's memorization skill. Facts do not do much good unless they are used for something. Besides, we are now in an age where we have easier access to more information than ever before. The obligation should be on schools to emphasize critical analysis and interpretation of facts rather than mass memorization.

The recall type of assessment doesn't enquire further into the student's creative and critical thinking aptitude since critical thinking is more than merely selecting from a set of given options.

While taking these types of tests, students don't need to show the reasoning behind the information or if they can apply that knowledge to different situations or if they can prove mastery of the subject using different information. By evaluating our young scholars in this way, we're not giving them enough opportunities to show their knowledge and we're not getting enough information about the limits of their understanding. If their assessments consist of only a recitation of facts and formulas, the method they undertake to study is equally bankrupt. Studying becomes nothing more than cramming—there is little, if any, engagement in the underlying issues beneath the information.

Fact-only testing can be used effectively as a preliminary evaluative tool, where short quizzes check whether students grasp of certain particulars or basic notions. Not used for grading purposes, it provides feedback for the teacher to see how they are transmitting these points and to ensure that students know the content needed for later interpretation.

We would like to see all major assessments written by the teacher. It is great when teachers use their opinions, life experiences, and strengths to shape what they teach and how they assess. It is a demonstration of an active interaction between the teacher and the academic material. Students become interested in the class and with learning when they see their instructor excited about the material. Standardized units and assessments depersonalize the classroom experience and create a less inviting environment for adults to educate and for students to learn. They can kill the passion.

The ideal method would be to evaluate how students use and interpret the material they have learned. Situations can be set up which motivate students to think imaginatively to solve a problem or come up with premises to reach conclusions. Perhaps students could explore the reasoning behind existing formulas and theses or investigate the potential applications of factual knowledge. Projects, essays, and real-world activities that compel the student to interact with the material are the best way to find out what students know. There is no question that administering this method is time-consuming, but it gives a clear picture of student understanding. Additionally, the process of taking this style of assessment also is an educational experience for students. Exams cease to exist as only a tool for teachers to get information. When the evaluation is meaningful, students do not view it as pointless, frightening or something to be avoided.

Assessments that are educational create a motivation for students to be inquisitive, to be comfortable with measuring their own growth, and to use that information for personal progress beyond the scope of their academic career.

COMPETITION AND COOPERATION

Competition is woven into the entire fabric of American life. It seems to exist everywhere we look, from our economic system to the entertainment industry. It is even a major part of many domestic structures where family members compete against each other for acceptance and love from parents, children, and siblings. There are places where competition can be appropriate, like in sports, and there are places where it is very inappropriate, like in the home. School, a place presently rife with competition, occupies a sort of middle ground; there are select situations in education where competition may be helpful and many others where it has no place.

Competition should never be built into the academic structure of a school. By this, we mean that students should not be forced to compete with or be compared to other students concerning grades or knowledge. A central reason for school is the education and celebration of the achievement of all students—not just the top. But that is exactly what happens when academically-slower students are judged against the so-called top students.

There are other problems. In academically competitive environments students are tasked to master the same material, irrespective of the needs of individual students. In so doing schools devalue self-knowledge and the path towards having self-knowledge. Academic competition and the grading system also encourages cheating. Students may feel they need to cheat and then rationalize it. When they leave formal education, dishonesty may become another common aspect of life that they will see as normal, or worse, necessary. Lastly, a culture of competition discourages collaborative work. A more appropriate and more fruitful school system is one that minimizes competition promotes collaboration, focuses on the education of all students, and urges students to pursue self-knowledge.

There are those who argue that competition positively motivates young people to do homework, master academic material, and regularly attend class. The fact that classroom competition and fear of failure within the school institution will motivate some students to do so is indisputable. However, the test is to see if it also fosters inquisitive individuals who will learn during their entire life and be encouraged to be a part of the human endeavor by creating more and more new experiences. Will they love learning? Will they know themselves well enough to seek out their own challenges and be self-disciplined? Unfortunately, many "successful" students with high grades are not inquisitive and intrinsically motivated. This system of competition can be addictive. In the future, they will likely act based on the rewards and punishments given by others. Pride and fear become their primary sources of motivation.

One of the purposes of schools is to prepare young people for the world after formal education. There are some who say that the world is competitive and cruel, and so it is best to use school to adjust young people to that fact. These debaters forget that first impressions last long after the initial meeting. Formal schooling is the first major interaction many of us have with organized society. If young people are surrounded by adults who implore cutthroat strategies that pit them against their peers, students will believe the world must operate in that way. Their lives follow what they experienced in their formative years. Teach cooperation and, in time, the world changes with it.

But let's go a step further. Not only is it a better way of social interaction, through collaborative projects we can gain more knowledge. When people collaborate it is in response to the realization that while I may hold one piece to a puzzle, it may be that someone else holds another and only together, using our individual skills and perspectives, can we fulfill our desires. This belief is not some empty "can't we all get along" rhetoric, but an acknowledgment of the possible benefits of mutual self-interest. The online world is full of successful cases of collaboration. One example is open source software. This manner of transparency and information-sharing accomplished through mutual self-interest can be effective in working on many other issues. Climate change research and medicine are just two fields that stand much to gain through emphasizing collaboration over competition. Schools can encourage this style and live it. There is much more to gain from an education system that deemphasizes competition over who can learn more and emphasizes cooperation and the education of all students.

INDOCTRINATION

When children first start out in life, they are told to trust their parents. This, of course, is a good thing. When they begin school, they are told to follow their teachers and to accept the ideas and rules of the classroom and the building. The theme in the early part of life is to follow and not to question. They are told to obey laws and to believe what they learn in their houses of worship. This command to do and think as you're told comes to them from all sides of our culture. Educators have a critical role to play in shaping how young people engage their world and in preventing them from being passive thinkers.

Unfortunately, for many adults, ideas are formulated by others and beliefs are cultivated by others to such a degree that they trust no explanation of reality not first framed by someone else. This applies to liberals, conservatives and those of all political stripes. People rarely examine the basis for positions they disagree with, and rarer still do they critically assess positions they agree with. We've become both a cynical and naïve country, and we get no benefit from either side. We distrust each other to almost mind-bogglingly pessimistic levels, but when it comes to examining the ideas of others, we are easily gulled into believing simplistic arguments. There are times when people feel they are thinking freely, but they are doing nothing more than picking between two sides of a coin. In these cases, the little critical faculty used is in choosing between the limited options put forward by someone else. Making those choices is not critical thinking, rather it is the most common and insidious form of indoctrination.

The process of imparting only a particular point of view—neither allowing for critical assessment nor fostering creativity—is indoctrination. Open academic discourse and the exchange of cultural perspectives do not exist alongside indoctrination. Indeed, no manner of thought is acceptable unless it falls within the instructor's ideological framework. It is not education, but nonetheless, this system of constricting the minds of others is often part of today's classroom experience. Teachers can do quite a bit to stem this by helping young people learn how to think for themselves while not fearing the ideas of others.

Teachers need to actively teach critical thinking and creativity—it is not enough to allow it in the classroom. Because of the subtle way indoctrination can slip into the teaching process, it is possible for teachers to be unintentionally guilty of indoctrination. Students can be shown how to seek various points of view, create their own hypotheses, and then evaluate the information. If students do not question material on their own volition, the teacher must demonstrate how critical thinking and creativity work by examining any position, even their own positions. Once students understand the process and begin to practice it, education will be fun and real learning will take place. There are those teachers who do not want the topics they have taught or the material they have assigned subjected to questioning. While most teachers know more facts and information than their students, we can all learn from each other when it comes to discussing personal perspectives and applying a critical lens to our understanding of the material. When teachers humble themselves and realize that we all can learn from each other, teaching becomes more fun for them as well.

School can even be a place where students learn the material through direct experience. For an example of this, imagine a middle school science class that incorporated constructing and studying a bioswale on school grounds. The class learned about natural ecosystems, geology, and indigenous plants, and maybe even, math, chemistry, and local history. In so doing they found real world uses for classroom lessons and learn from their experiences. They were not restricted to obtaining all their information from a secondary source such as a book or their instructor. They did not memorize "right answers". This direct experience approach applies to all subjects. In math and science, students learn the process of solving problems by using formulas, but unfortunately often have little idea the logic behind the method or what real world applications that particular math may have. It is not enough to come up with the correct answers. Young people should investigate the process that forced the answer, and moreover, how the questions came to be asked and how their responses can be found in everyday life. Mathematics is all around us; it can be the most beautifully relevant class a student takes. Our students can interact with math with purpose and curiosity. This principle applies to all courses and all information presented to students.

Every school that values critical thinking, creativity, an open academic discourse and an exchange of cultural perspectives should do everything in their power to eliminate indoctrination. For although information is important to know, without evaluating that information what remains is indoctrination.

SELF-KNOWLEDGE

Much of this book tries to teach young people how to gain self-knowledge. It is a critical part of maturation for self-knowledge allows an individual to be better prepared to select appropriate challenges and meet them. Having it gives confidence, independence, and helps with critical, creative thinking. In short, it allows a person to guide their life. Self-knowledge is the knowledge of what you can do (i.e. knowledge of capability) and the knowledge of the purpose of what you want to do (i.e. knowledge of desire and the motivations for having that desire) in particular situations. A person pursuing self-knowledge must also ask if they foresee personal growth by undertaking the challenge.

Most students, those with high as well as low grades, consign themselves to being defined by someone else. When these students make statements like "I am good at math," or "I am not a good runner," they are usually basing their views on what teachers, parents, and peers have told them. Their opinions are not based on their self-knowledge. In school, students are in an environment where they rarely create their situations and select and pursue their challenges. It is difficult (if not impossible) to gain self-knowledge when this is the case. For schools to motivate young people to make an inquiry into themselves (both of abilities and desires) there should be an environment where young people choose their challenges and examine their abilities.

Let us turn to a fictional example of a young person in a modern American high school who creates a path towards gaining self-knowledge. A young woman who has never played sports finds herself with a desire to be an excellent long-distance runner and so she chooses to join the cross-country team. By selecting a challenge and by creating a situation she is now in a position to assess her ability as well as to gain knowledge of her desires and the motivations for having those desires. She knows what she wants to do (be a talented long-distance runner), and she knows why she wants to do it (let's say to gain better physical fitness and reduce stress), and in her assessment, by pursuing this challenge she will have greater control of other facets of her life and it will create good future challenges as well. She feels that being a good runner will open up other avenues for growth. What she does not know is her ability—we must be careful here in noting that it is not what she guesses her ability to be, or what she feels her ability is, or even what she wants her ability to be—but her knowledge of her ability. She does not know if she is a good long-distance runner. The question now before her is, "How do I learn what my ability is and how do I reach my goal of being a great long-distance runner?" She must experiment. Experimentation, both within a challenge and in the pursuit of different challenges, is a necessary part of gaining self-knowledge.

As she practices with her teammates, she notices that she is faster than some and slower than others. She also observes that there is a group of girls who take to the track every day with no other purpose than to be the fastest person on the team. She also notices other runners who do not run very fast and do not try to run fast; they are content to jog along at a pace that appears to be below that of which they are capable. But the young woman in our example is new to the team and has no friends as of yet, so she runs by herself setting her own pace. In running along, she reminds herself of her goal to be a great long-distance runner. Every day she takes note of her time and of when she got tired and when she had little bursts of energy. She experiments to maximize the periods of additional energy and minimize those where it's absent. She struggles to improve her time and doesn't place too much concern about those who remain faster than her. She's dissatisfied because she thinks it's possible for her to run faster but so far it hasn't happened.

Her focus is her own fastest time, what her coach calls her personal record. Her goal every day is to improve her fastest time. She doesn't worry about setting the record for the team because she assesses that for now, that would be an inappropriate challenge, something clearly beyond her capability. Appropriate challenges are challenges the individual can maneuver in—ones in which students will not easily master, but can. Appropriate challenges are the situations which give us the greatest self-knowledge. It is irrelevant for our example if this student ever becomes the fastest member of her cross-country team or the fastest in the state. She found an appropriate challenge and joining the team was a fruitful endeavor because she exercised self-discipline and gained self-knowledge. And likely, she will be more willing to pursue other challenges in the future and be better prepared to meet them.

The process our long-distance runner underwent, of seeking her own challenges and creating her own situations, should be taught by all teachers in all classrooms. Learning the skill of how to obtain self-knowledge will stay with the student for a lifetime.

Self-knowledge is a knowing of the spirit within.

PERSONAL RESPONSIBILITY

At every moment we are all capable of doing many different things. Amongst all of the possibilities that exist for us at any one moment, we choose one action and reject others. Some of our actions are the result of instantaneous selections, and others are the product of a long deliberative process. These choices we make—both of what to do and what we chose not to—have effects. Having personal responsibility means reflecting on your actions and your choices, facing the consequences, and if need be, doing differently in the future. Part of schooling can be an education in the ownership of our lives.

Having it is one of the best learning experiences one can have. More than just living a questioned life—having a sense of personal responsibility means living an active life, and accepting the belief that you can create what you want and that you own what you create.

Just as certain ways of thinking make people more motivated to be personally responsible, other thoughts do the opposite. When a person feels that they are disconnected from their actions, as well as from other people and the world, or that they are unable to do what they would like, or that their actions have no effect, then there is less motivation to have personal responsibility. These feelings of separation and limitation are the two biggest roadblocks to having ownership of one's actions. When an individual falls into this mentality, they maintain a passive distance from their actions and unburden themselves from the pursuit of personal responsibility–both at school and beyond. It is as if they have become a spectator in their own life.

Countering these feelings requires a certain amount of willfulness. The best course of action is to take greater freedom to experiment and choose, and in turn, have more opportunities to see the effects of their actions.

Administrators should enable and encourage teachers to be empowered in this way. Whether that empowerment comes from creating their curriculum, bringing their life experiences to their teaching, working with their peers on projects they created, or participating in programs beyond the classroom, the goal is for educators to immerse themselves as choosing agents in their professional lives. This can apply to all adults in the building—counselors, janitors, cooks—everyone. When administrators entrust their staff with being active in the school community, all adults in the building feel that they are part of their school and their school is part of them.

With students, the situation is slightly different, yet the feelings of disconnection and limitation are very real problems. Teachers have the ability to show young people how to make more connections and how to have more power. Students can exercise control over their lives by making their own decisions and not to relying on teachers and counselors to do so for them. For example, this could be done by choosing their own classes and how they use their free time. And these students, in having the strength to take risks and the willingness to explore new possibilities, will keep an open mind when others do the unexpected and understand that through experimentation we grow. They should see their successes and their errors, be shown how to be accountable and how to take ownership of their actions.

Our education system can be a place where we encourage an active participation in life and never limitations. Young people can develop an awareness of what needs to be done—and the wherewithal to do it. Whether that means starting a much-needed volunteer organization or picking up a bit of litter, they can take the initiative and have a sense of personal responsibility to improve their—and everyone's—quality of life. Young people need not be raised in a society where too many problems are written off as "other people's faults" and too many tasks are neglected as being "not my job," where we don't take up the important tasks, even though we hope someone else will. It is easy to forget how interconnected we all are and how much each of us can do. The American anthropologist Margaret Mead is quoted to have remarked that we can "Never doubt that a small group of thoughtful, committed citizens can change the world. Indeed, it is the only thing that ever has."

Learning how your actions affect others requires opportunities to try, fail, and try again in another way. A great life is one that takes the freedom to choose and appreciates the potential residing in responsibility.

BEING A GOOD STUDENT

Being a good student is an active process. It is not a stage in life in which one can rest, nor is there a list of outside designations necessary to be a good student. Rather, being a good student is an attitude—it is the relationship an individual has with the world around them.

While every student is different and will construct their surroundings based on their particular circumstance, young people who have the attitude of a good student have many of the following dispositions and perspectives: they go to school to learn to think and interpret. They focus on topics that enliven the human spirit and love learning for learning's sake. They want to learn more about the world within them and their world beyond. They are never complacent and are always curious. They don't feel that they have to attend school simply because someone else thinks they must and they don't graduate in order to have a certain career simply because someone else wants them to have that job. Good students are engaged in their life. They take responsibility for their actions. Good students do whatever is necessary to make the class interesting. They force discussions and cultivate a critical mind by questioning their instructor and classmates. If a teacher does not cooperate, they do it anyway. There is nothing more boring than to sit in a classroom with a blank mind and stare at the wall for an entire class period.

Having this attitude, they realize that learning about the human experience enriches our understanding of who we are, how we got here, and where we are going. And most importantly, the learning of past experiences increases their interest in and desire for creating more and more new experiences. An education is a foundation for self-growth: as a member of a community and as an individual.

It is possible for everyone to be a good student.

TEXTBOOKS

Disappointingly little real education takes place when schools choose to use only textbooks. By 'textbook,' we mean the primary written material for a class (usually the only book used), purchased by the school board by contract for use in all classrooms (and so, is not chosen by the teacher). For the most part, textbooks fail to live up to their potential. Far too often textbooks create more problems than they solve.

Now, there's little wrong with having a book that acts as a resource for general information, but there is a significant problem when it is not the starting place of the class but the ending place. When textbooks are the only written source in the classroom, the textbook monopolizes the syllabus, and the primary goal of a course may become little more than "getting through" that text. Textbooks cover a wide span of material, and while it's up to educators to find and emphasize the important issues, ineffective teachers don't often take it upon themselves to do so. In this way, less ambitious teachers become handmaidens to textbooks, and through textbooks, can slide through their careers dependent on the information presented in district-issued books. Other aspects are equally disconcerting, such as the reality that having only one source does little to engender critical and comparative thought.

An American history textbook is a perfect example to illustrate the point. The story of history depends on the perspective of the individual telling their interpretation of previous events. The story of our civil war when written by a southern economic historian might well differ from that described by a northern social historian. Something written during the Reconstruction about the war is going to be different from one written in the last decade. It is important not only who writes, but when and why. In many textbooks, specific sections are anonymously written. Neither the teacher nor the student has any information about the author. Students need to learn to analyze possible motivations of an author, but the current format robs students of the opportunity to do so. We need more sources to allow comparison and allow students an opportunity to get more information and perspectives.

One might ask, "Why can't textbooks put forward an objectively true explanation of the past?" They can't because there is none. Explanations depend on who is stating them, where and when they are stating them, and why. When students are given only one reading of a complex issue, not only are they losing out on information, but moreover, they are missing out on learning the lesson that information is the result of opinions—and opinions sometimes vary. Students must get beyond the idea that knowledge is something that can be culled without interaction like some word from an inert dictionary.

The problems continue. Textbooks, across the disciplines, intentionally and unintentionally, also present inaccurate understandings on the structure and acquisition of knowledge. They enforce a linear concept of progress where A necessarily led to B which inevitably led to C, all in the steady forward march of time. In so doing, the book ignores the failures, debates, dead ends, confusions and changes that those physicists, politicians, mathematicians, and literary giants themselves underwent. This creates an incorrect—and intimidating—vision of how knowledge is gained and may not motivate young people to freely engage themselves as an active member in this never ending process. Rarely do textbooks allow students to see broad connections and interrelations between academic disciplines, thereby demonstrating that all subjects are on a continuum of other subjects. The study of physics overlaps with the study of chemistry, philosophy with mathematics, literature and politics, biology and ethics, and so on.

There are those in public education who like textbooks. Some believe that they are a definitive compilation of all important points, and others state that they are a time saver for teachers when planning a syllabus. There are those who lobby for its use out of convenience since one book is cheaper to buy than many. These are poor excuses. They are made by those who don't know the subject matter well, teachers who don't create their own curriculum, and apologists for a government that chooses not to budget enough money for a school to purchase the correct written materials.

It's true that the quality of textbooks is improving and now there are humanities books which present complex issues, multiple perspectives, and urge the student to think about the issue and not just memorize information from its pages. There are science and math books that provide context and urge the student to engage the material actively. We acknowledge this is occurring and we applaud this shift. But even when the textbook is great, there is still another problem which is the format. The format creates a psychological barrier, for when one book is put before students as the book with all the answers, it creates an impression that knowledge can be accumulated objectively and can be extracted without interaction—it removes the student's duty to analyze.

In the humanities, a better method would be to have the teacher select a series of primary or secondary sources reflecting various aspects of the subject because all matters depend on the interpretations given them. If we keep with the previous example, imagine a section on the Reconstruction era in American history. It could be studied by having the students read an essay on the subject by a northern business person, and another by a southern farmer. Perhaps a speech given by a northern congressman could be compared to another by a southern politician. Reading about the daily life of an ex-slave could be followed by one on the everyday struggles of a northern factory worker. Writings by indigenous peoples, women's groups, those traveling west, different President's opinions, and others could be included as well. Views of economists, social historians, and other contemporary academics certainly could be a part of the section. The context of those events would be illuminated and the viewpoints would be different. Because of that, the student would obtain a better and truer picture of that period and the issues involved. All aspects of history could be examined this way.

This practice of engaging the material is not restricted to social studies and can also be applied to other subjects. English, math, biology, and every other department can adopt it to varying degrees. Biology courses, for example, could discuss the context of hypotheses and scientific discoveries along with the desired methods and goals of those leading thinkers. It would be helpful for math and physics classes to go beyond stating equations and rules, to explaining why they are the way they are and ask what their ramifications might be. As young people are exposed to multiple written sources from multiple perspectives, they begin to see that everything is controversial—that there are no objective truths.

This method is equally successful in all classes, not just with the brightest or oldest students. Everyone is capable of this way of thinking. Schools cannot speed up the natural process of learning by avoiding the experimentation, imagining, playing, trying of new ideas, and grappling with foreign concepts that are necessary to master complicated concepts and issues. When educators make the decision to fill their class time with reading facts from textbooks, they are doing a disservice to young people, for no student will learn anything aside from how to memorize and regurgitate.

The process we propose does not simplify the educational process but complicates it. Much of the information imparted in today's schools is easy to teach and easy for the student to understand, but it is simplified to the point of being inaccurate.

The critics of our method say that it only confuses students. We should all be so lucky. The textbook method teaches students to accept what is written as fact, and more than that, it teaches them not to think but to accept. We ought to encourage the process of listening, thinking, and evaluating, and not blindly taking what is popularly said. This process would create a public of creative thinkers who seek out other perspectives, communicate with each other, and are active in the world in which they live—and that is what education ought to have been doing all along. In our modern world, to not seek is to fall behind. We cannot afford to have our young people passive in the world around them.

CLASS CHOICE

Choosing their classes can be a part of a young person's path to greater self-knowledge and seeking appropriate challenges. Schools have a rich opportunity to coach young scholars and offer advice.

Students should be able to enroll in classes above or below their past academic achievements. When a student who took one class at a particular level is required to stay at that same level in the future, it can create elitism in the advanced students and feelings of self-doubt, hesitancy, and depressed worth in students forced into lower-level classes. These feelings originate when an outside authority figure imposes their presumption over and denies the individual's own assessment based on self-knowledge. The administrator who tracks students may believe that the low-tracked student rarely improves beyond their track and the high-tracked student will never find themselves needing closer academic supervision. Moreover, this adult likely believes that no young person knows themselves well enough to select their own appropriate challenges. The educational system from beginning to end should be open to all students.

Every school can have a range of classes that reflect the variety of academic skills present in the student body: classes for students who have academic challenges such as reading difficulties, and others for students who have demonstrated advanced learning skills. In between, there may be classes for the young person who is not in need of remedial work, but just the same, is not yet ready to master complex skills. And when class sizes are small enough this can occur within the same classroom.

The first step in making all courses open to anyone is increased communication between adults and students before the course begins. Time should be set aside for teachers and counselors to familiarize incoming students with the material covered in prospective classes and offer placement suggestions based on the adult's insight into an individual student's academic ability. However, the student makes the final decision. This not only instills responsibility but leaves possibilities open for the student to try to advance up the academic ladder. If they wish to try their hand at more challenging classes or don't want to take advanced classes, schools should allow it.

In the typical structure, this amount of student choice might seem problematic. It could potentially lead to students attending classes below their academic ability, which is not so good. The students that don't challenge themselves and knowingly take classes below their capability are often doing so out of a belief that since they stand a better chance of receiving a higher grade in an easier class that it is not worth the risk of taking a more difficult class. In this way, grades are propagating the very culture of mediocrity that grades are supposed to eliminate. Right now, so too exist other young people who choose to push themselves by taking a chance on succeeding in advanced classes and are willing to risk only sometimes doing well. This group, by being choosing agents who have surely gained more self-knowledge and more knowledge about a challenging topic, is not rewarded where it supposedly counts, in the grade book. If schools eliminate grades young people will be far less motivated to take classes below their ability and not punished for making a decision on how far they can go. Moreover, this is another reason why everyone would be better served with more electives and a shorter course length. Both would create more opportunities for student experimentation and reassessment. For example, someone could choose a class and then adjust their next trimester or semester's course selection based on how the first one went. Doing so, the administration doesn't lock students into a potentially bad choice for a year.

It is better to make school a place where the students take what classes they desire, and the adults teach responsibility for actions.

ATTENDANCE

Attendance is invaluable, because what can occur in class is without replacement. In a great classroom, there are discussions, debates, and cooperative learning essential to education. No out-of-class project or essay can substitute them. And so, what can occur in the class will not occur when a student works alone. Everyone in the education profession knows this and so schools require attendance. But this is not the end of the story. Rather it is the beginning.

Administrators and teachers require attendance not only for the above reasons but also because of the belief that the discipline of coming to class every day is good for students. However, discipline without purpose is control. What is implicit in their assumptions—and the origin of a fundamental problem in attendance policy—is the belief that teachers are always presenting something worthwhile in their classrooms. Sadly, this is not true and out-of-touch with the on-the-ground reality. Many teachers have failed to make attending class worthwhile for students. When an instructor cannot provide an interesting creative purpose to the class time, why should dozens of students be forced to waste away in classrooms that more resemble a holding tank than a house of education? Teachers must provide something unique during this time that students cannot receive beyond those walls.

Class time spent covering new material and in discussion can create a learning community.

A number of issues are emerging in this discussion. Ideally students should attend every class and teachers should use their time in meaningful ways, but unfortunately, both students and teachers aren't always holding up their end of the bargain. Schools are faced with issues of administrative compulsion as well as the freedom of choice and movement by students. Mandatory attendance is a complicated matter and cannot be solved by additional rules or a firmer hand by administrators.

The natural action for a young person who feels that in-class time is a waste is to either silently come to class and dissolve like a gray fog into the seat, or to simply not to come. Either way, the student won't present their suggestions or concerns to the teacher—because the entire academic environment urges against a student critiquing a teacher. When a student stares at a wall all period or skips because the class is a waste, nobody wins. The teacher would benefit from hearing from this student.

It is incumbent upon the teacher to begin a new relationship with their students and take it upon themselves to motivate their students to be positive in their activism. Great in-class time should be a joint goal of teachers and students, and this involves an open conversation from all sides, a lack of complacency and authoritarianism, and a willingness for all parties to listen and change. Rather, the teacher must be vocal in telling young people that in this classroom the students' first reaction should be to bring their grievances to the educator, and moreover, it should be known that their complaints will be heard and responded to.

The students have the right to a good class, and when they don't get it, they have the responsibility not to be complacent. They have a right to be active in their education. When this type of relationship is established between teachers and an active and responsive student body it is natural for the attendance to be very high.

There remains an unresolved problem. It stems from a hypocritical policy most schools maintain. They issue platitudes on the importance of in-class time and mandatory attendance, but then belie the value of class time by also permitting late-term solo projects and extra credit. This practice allows students to skip class and still pass. Truant students blow off attending classes until the last part of the term, foresee their low grades, and in a panic, push for a last-minute reprieve. Teachers usually give it. Today's students are sermonized on attending every class, but the institutional structure allows the student to flatly break it without repercussions. These extra-credit projects reinforce the prevalent belief that the classroom community is of little value and the grade is the only indicator of learning. We have a system that coddles students who flounder in schools, learn nothing, and rarely attend. Their final record shows academic success, but it is nothing more than a smokescreen. Through this, young people learn unacceptable lessons: they do not have to come to class to get passing grades, and passing grades are tantamount to education. Not only does this teach that the grade is more important than the material of the course, worse still, it teaches irresponsibility. It devalues the educational content of the class lectures, discussions, and cooperative learning. You cannot substitute good class time with make-up work outside of class, period.

This discussion on extra-credit should be an unnecessary one. If we did not give grades, a discussion on extra-credit is moot. If students don't attend class and complete the requirements, they cannot experience the totality of the course; if they fail to experience the course—extra-credit or not—isn't that consequence enough?

The lasting solution to increasing classroom attendance lies in three parts. One, we need to hire good teachers, improve the mediocre, and fire the bad. Two, we need teachers to take it upon themselves to have a conversation with students about in-class time, and administrators need to urge teachers to have this discussion. Three, we also need to have an infrastructure that does not subvert the proper emphasis on attending class.

EXTRACURRICULAR ACTIVITIES

So much growth occurs when a school has a great extracurricular program. Extracurricular activities are the ecstatic acts of life which allow young people to play and mature. Not merely appealing to the child within our students by enlivening their daily lives, these activities expand their worldview and provide exposure to new areas of exploration and ideas not covered in the regular school curriculum. They can lead to future hobbies and careers while presently developing a good member of society. They act as mediums for maturation and independence, establish a sense of ownership and place, build communities, and foster care for fellow humans. Students gain feelings of competency and self-worth when they are involved and responsible for something meaningful. Without these activities, students would probably feel that attending school would be like going to a bad job.

There are some who dismiss extracurricular activities as the least important part of the school. Deemed an unnecessary expense, their funding often gets eliminated. For most young people these recreational experiences can sometimes be more educational than class since they permit the playing, experimenting and imagining involved for deep learning. Moreover, for those young people who are having trouble at home or in the community, participating in extracurricular activities can be a means for those students to address and work on their problems—it can become a real type of psychological therapy.

Extracurriculars should not be required or be related to grades or credit but based solely on the interest of the student. This permits students to be a bit more liberal in their selection and to experiment in choosing activities. In class, many of our young people are under so much stress to succeed that they only engage in that which they know they will do well. They don't experiment. They don't take risks. They don't try new things. It is a tragedy to reject educational experiences out of fear, and yet, many young people determine their course load in just that way. The only time they stop prejudging themselves is when venturing into an arena that they feel they can experiment without being under the pressure of grades and credit.

Many of the aspirations we have for the education system are met through the benefits of extracurricular activities. They provide a critical part of the learning process and should be standard in every school.

INDIVIDUALIZED LEARNING

There are great individual differences among our students. Some students are more mature than others; some are more ready for particular subjects than their peers; some students have learning difficulties; and others, for whatever reason, do not find the material relevant to their lives. All of these affect whether or not the students will absorb the material in any course.

Schools and school districts can address this issue of individual differences as a foundational matter of policy. When a student lacks the opportunity to learn the course material in a way that is meaningful to them, it is likely that they won't learn it at all. It is up to the school to provide an environment in which every young person has the chance to pursue their own challenges and can engage the subject in different ways When this happens, young people gain greater academic knowledge in addition to becoming more active participants in life.

To illustrate the near comic difficulty in expecting all students to learn about a subject by doing the same assignment we turn to the rather famous story from the School for Animals. There, as in most schools, all of the animals were required to do the same work. On the fourth day of science class, the topic was flight. The teacher felt that the best way for these young animals to learn about flight was to fly. Since all students were to be graded on this assignment, all the animals gathered at a massive tower. The animals were told to walk up the ramp to the top of the 50-foot tower. As they stood on the platform, the eagle was told to jump off and show the class how it was done. He did so and soared and glided to the field below. His grade was an A. Next up was the elephant. He questioned the advisability of the jump. Not only would the elephant not learn to fly, but he would be injured in the process and probably be a more unwilling participant in future assignments. The elephant's impediment to that assignment was physical. With our human students, the differences are equally as great, but we cannot see them as plainly. Those differences are intellectual, cultural, social and psychological. And this means that what is good for the whole class is not one assignment for the whole class: there are many different ways to teach the academic material.

It would be unnecessarily burdensome for a teacher to set up a different assignment for each student and time would never permit it. However, it would not be difficult for the teacher to present to the class four or six options to complete a particular assignment and allow the student, depending on their interest, to determine which to do. When this happens, interest and morale rise and there is an ownership on the part of the student towards that assignment and learning in general. Along with the given list, the teacher can leave the assignment open for a student to construct their own activity with the teacher's approval. This way, the student could practice creativity and design coursework related to the classroom material that would be their own and geared to their current interests.

Not only can there be options for individuals within a class, but also options for individualized classes. That is, if a student shows interest and motivation towards a particular subject, educators should encourage them to explore that topic by designing their own course, like an independent study, service project, or in-depth research. Given these options, students can come up with many ways to learn that are substantial enough to warrant

Individualized learning

receiving credit.

All of this can happen after students have been taught how to direct their learning. Much of this book seeks to put young people in a position where they can have this ability. By encouraging self-knowledge and self-discipline, by eliminating fear and competition against others academically, and by allowing experimentation and giving meaningful feedback, along with other things, schools can actively teach the next generation how to engage with their inquisitive self.

When there is a choice, interest and achievement go way up. When students are examining a topic from a variety of perspectives, classroom discussion becomes more open and oral reports more interesting. This tends to eliminate competition and naturally leads to cooperation on assignments. Another benefit is that students will realize that because interpretation is always present, there is no objective way to look at any subject.

Good teachers do not say "That is the truth," but choose to allow the student the opportunity to find the truth and its manifestations through their actions.

SYLLABUS

In many schools, the first thing a student is handed on day one of a new class is the syllabus. Written by the teacher, it states the broad academic topics covered during the semester, the goals for the course, and the assessment structure. Up to that point, nearly all student knowledge about the class and teacher was based on conversations with classmates enrolled in previous terms. It was hearsay and remembrances; now they are handed something directly from their new instructor. But the real benefit of the syllabus is not as a harbinger of future events, but in its potential role as a conversation starter.

The best part about a syllabus might not be what is written, but what is said. Teachers who value the power of meaningful communication immediately begin a relationship with their students. While distributing the syllabus, these instructors express how they want the class to run and inform students what they should expect from the course. Exams and disciplinary arrangements are spelled out, and students are told how they will be evaluated. Teachers can also state their educational philosophy. Any opinions they have about cooperative learning and student feedback are made clear from the beginning. This sort of transparency is vital to building a climate of trust. But it is not only a matter of reading out loud what is written in the syllabus. A first impression is made through the way it is said. A teacher who wishes to create a climate of mutual respect and a lack of fear must also encourage their students to speak freely about their wants and needs for the class. The teacher can show through action that in this course there will be a dialogue.

Despite all these benefits, or perhaps because of all these possibilities, beginning the student-teacher relationship 'the right way' is a cause of stress for teachers. The written syllabus is a tool to explain the structure and attitude of the course, however, it cannot create or predict the future. It is important for teachers not to confuse being prepared with having planned day-to-day lessons far in advance. Some instructors, especially new ones, become nervous in the classroom and by wanting to be certain that class time will be full and enjoyable, they try to map out every day's lesson months prior, or even before the academic year begins. These teachers have such good intentions. They want every day to be fun and educational. They want their students to know what their class will cover. They don't want to leave anything out.

Teachers shouldn't worry so much. And they shouldn't presume that because something is written on the calendar it has to happen. Teaching requires adaptability and success in this profession requires being able to adjust. Perhaps a certain topic is taking longer than expected or students have expressed interest in a relevant concept that is not in the syllabus. A teacher must respond to this and not ignore it. Great things can happen in a classroom when it is flexible, open, responsive, and organic, just like real learning. Teachers shouldn't chip the syllabus in granite, but rather chip it in sand. Teachers will not only have less stress but also put themselves in a better position to respond to the class' needs.

There is one suggestion we would like to make to educators who want to be flexible in what they teach but don't know how. A teacher could make a list for themselves of the next five lessons they want to cover. Teach the first two. After that, rewrite a new list of five based off of existing lesson plans, student feedback, and any new concepts that arose in the process of teaching the first two. Again they teach the first two items on their list and continue this method through throughout the year. This allows the teacher to respond to student interest yet control the direction of the course and the material the teacher wants to instruct. It is a working balance between spontaneity and planning. It is also a time saver for teachers. No longer do they have to create unrealistic year-long lesson plans and then find themselves caught in a dilemma between satisfying the needs of the class and teaching the prepared curriculum.

EVERYDAY LIFE

Young people need to enjoy their years as students. Not only are the activities that bring joy to our lives themselves very educational, but an enjoyable daily life makes one curious about the world and more desirous of learning. A great everyday life is the key to a successful student. Sadly, for far too many of America's students' daily life is a painfully heartbreaking, alienating and discouraging affair. Too often schools focus on academically preparing children for their later years in life at the expense of anything else, and too rarely administrators write policy with the intention of making the present life enjoyable. Many of the problems discussed in this book are created when policy makers and educators fail to focus on the lives of students. What we are calling for is not more fun and games, but a demand for all young people to experience the bliss that comes with being an active participant in their lives. This joy can come in many ways. It comes when students are encouraged to establish their situations and abandon what ceases to be useful to them. It comes when students have the freedom to find appropriate challenges in academic and extracurricular pursuits, and when students have ownership of their choices and actions. It happens when young people take their ability to do things in the "real world" now—not just later.

Preparing children for their later years at the expense of their life now inadvertently creates a kind of confusion in students.

These young people have an identity shaped by the split role: their current self and the role of who they will be. Both of these selves, present and future, are in many cases more the creation of outside opinion such as parents, teachers, and friends rather than the individual's own internal self-assessment. At a time when people are just beginning to consider identity questions, they should be given the space and the ability to experiment and try new things. They should be encouraged to gain self-knowledge and learn who they are. Young people are not only our future, but they are also our present. Perhaps we should begin every day by asking students what they want to be today, rather than what they want to be when they grow up.

Schools must take a hard look at themselves. They must examine their institutional attitudes and methods, for these fundamental aspects affect the everyday life of both students and educators. Many policy changes are surface modifications that leave the underlying personality and structure wholly unchanged. Once schools change their priorities and start with an emphasis on today, they will dramatically improve students' lives, and in turn, their education. A great everyday life teaches many valuable lessons and creates a desire to learn more.

CONTENT AND LASTING LESSONS

The lessons we learn in school stay with us throughout our life—but they are not always the lessons our instructors expected. The facts and figures lectured in school are quickly forgotten. Data memorized for quizzes and tests fade into the recesses of the brain after the exams have passed.

But, for many young people their comprehensive conception of the world and humanity's relation to it, formed during the early years of life, will stay with them until they die. During the first decade or so of schooling, the foremost process the mind undertakes is not learning specific points and a description of their parts and properties, but rather attempting to create a map of the connective space between these points and attempting to come to grips with patterns seen. The lasting lesson from K-12 is in how the individual interacts with the world; it is one of relations, not of content. For most young people once this understanding is established, once they feel that they know "the way the world and people work" it becomes the most unassailable position they hold. It is the foundation for future structures. It is the sieve through which they filter new concepts. All information learned later in life, all content, will undergo inspection by their position.

Schools can emphasize this reality. That is not to say that schools teach less material or have less academic rigor, but that they have an appreciation for the opportunity to positively affect young people's understanding of the world and their connection to it. By having this appreciation, teachers can improve the lives of students, and society as a whole.

Lifelong curiosity and a positive relationship with learning can be created by instructing young people how to think rather than what to think. The emphasis here is on the process of teaching students how to seek and acquire information for themselves. It is only the secondary objective for students to learn the content that is the result. When students know how to think and how to obtain information, and then how to process and filter it, they have learned a method which will stay with them for a lifetime.

Relations can also be imparted through manner and attitude. By teaching classes using love, cooperation, empathy, and all other thematic concepts of this book, by having the everyday life of school saturated with these themes, by removing negative aspects such as fear and undue competition, schools can create a positive image of how the world works that is new and foreign to previous generations. Once it exists in their minds, in time, it will exist in all of society. We should never underestimate the ability society has of changing itself.

ELECTIVES

Our young people live in a different world than previous generations. Through the internet, they already have easier access to so much information, and after graduation they will be more likely to have multiple careers, have more opportunities to travel, and will be more likely to interact with people different from them (even right in their neighborhood). Tomorrow will be an exciting time for young people.

Right now, however, since far too many schools have a curriculum of only required courses, the class options are so narrow that students graduate with a very parochial, often inaccurate, understanding of the world—one far too limited for this expanding society of ours. Electives, or non-required classes, might be the means to eliminate that problem by presenting students with a variety of topics and a greater discourse surrounding academic subjects. By expanding their education into subjects ordinarily unavailable, schools seize the opportunity to give young people a general knowledge of and an interest in many subjects. Breadth and depth are very beneficial for those whose schooling ends with the twelfth grade and are a necessity for students pursuing college.

Teachers also stand to gain from an expanded curriculum. By leading unique classes, they have greater control over the content and so will be urged to develop a course in their vision. By crafting a syllabus tailored to their students' specific needs, teachers can remain flexible and change the material as the term progresses. All good teachers love to be creative with the students and to have the opportunity to share their passion for a subject. Both parties will profit from more options and variety.

One good way to combine a required curriculum with an elective program is to break up the required curriculum into separate courses or parts. For example, most high schools in the country require at least one year of United States history. That requirement could be met by breaking up a year-long course into a number of one-term or one-semester electives, each teaching a section of United States history. Perhaps some could focus on an issue or theme while others are divided into chronological periods. Some could be more challenging than others. We have seen this done with great results where many students liked the breakdown and took two to three additional classes out of interest. Choice is better than force. Just as this concept applies to adults, it also applies to adolescents.

When students are allowed to select their classes they will find those that are relevant to their lives, and in turn, take ownership of their course load. Their motivation to regularly attend and learn critically increases. When young people realize that they possess the ability to make selections and set goals, that lesson will continue with them well beyond the schoolhouse door. These students will be choosing and active agents in their lives for years to come.

There is no question that having a rich and broad elective program makes more work for teachers. Planning and leading diverse courses will require an increase in their out-of-class preparation.Nonetheless, they should be the norm in every school, even those with a limited budget and number of instructors.

It is disappointing that schools now find themselves with limited funding. When money is short, classes get cut. The shop, art, music, theater, and athletics classes tend to be the first to go. Academic electives are never far behind, leaving only the state and district-required courses. And there we are again with our students, even "the best and the brightest," graduating with an unsophisticated view of the planet on which they live. It is so unfortunate that the government forces public schools into a position where the curriculum constricts young people's ability to understand and engage their modern world.

When a school accepts the opportunity to push its young scholars beyond a prescribed path, young people begin to understand that the beautiful and complex world in which they live is best seen through its variety.

UNSTRUCTURED TIME

When schools regularly allot time during the school day when students don't have scheduled classes or activities, young people learn a great lesson of lasting importance. This unstructured time possesses advantages over a tightly scheduled school day and free time after school cannot be substituted for free time in school.

Unstructured time allows for increased opportunities for one-on-one communication between students and teachers. Rarely will in-class time permit a student to approach a teacher to talk or for a teacher to informally discuss an issue with a student. Usually, the period is overfull—too many students and too much material. When this is compounded by a schedule full of classes and after-school obligations, literally, there is no time to talk. The give and take of ideas and unfettered conversations that young people can have with adults, as well as those between peers constitute the educational endeavor.

Too often in the current system, extra time is only allowed for making up exams and assignments from sick days or for those matters in which the student may need remedial help. We should give children the extra time to work on what they are good at and enjoy doing. By permitting students to seek out their own challenges and create their own situations, schools are encouraging real development. In this way, the natural process of learning by experimenting, imagining, playing, trying new ideas and grappling with foreign concepts necessary for mastering complicated concepts and issues is not only tacitly acknowledged, but is actively promoted through the allotment of school time.

Giving the students the space to learn in this way also requires adult involvement. Young people should be given the opportunity to choose how they spend this time but then held accountable for how they do so. Educators love speaking about student responsibility, but few permit its exercise—more often than not, individual teachers and the school infrastructure shield students from making choices and from the consequences of their decisions. In turn, many young people graduate high school with a poor understanding of the correlation between the actions they took and the results they experienced. Part of the power of unstructured time is teaching responsibility by giving students the experience of having to be responsible.

There are two major opposing arguments against having unstructured time in school and neither outweigh the benefits. The first is that kids are not capable of managing their own time and when left to their own devices young people will run roughshod over the classes in session. The second argument for a tightly scheduled day is safety. If the student is always in a structured environment, then the teachers and administrators always know what the students are doing and where they are, and can keep kids safe.

Both arguments have merit, but those concerns can be assuaged by making the liberties extended during unstructured time equal to the age level. While perhaps it would be silly to say that second graders should get a few hours a day to go wherever they want in the building and do whatever strikes their fancy, it is not absurd to allow those same students to have some in-class time to do as they please. Likewise, high school students should have freedom of movement and the ability to choose how they spend their time—requiring their presence in attending a "free period" classroom (like many home room classes) is as silly as turning eight-year-olds loose. Regardless of the age, schools should never punish the whole student body for the small percentage who cannot handle unstructured time. Learning to have the self-discipline to use their time can be very hard and it is not without its challenges and risks of individual setbacks. But no young person will quickly adapt to life after secondary education if they remain tethered for twelve years of school. It is at its best when it is different things at different age levels, and good teachers know what level of permissibility is educational for their students.

Unstructured time can be supremely educational when on the path toward having self-discipline and self-knowledge.

SELF-DISCIPLINE

Self-discipline is an individual using their mental power to control their actions for the purpose of self-improvement. By practicing self-discipline, young people gain a great deal of control, and thus a great deal of freedom. Moreover, having self-discipline is needed for the pursuit of self-knowledge, a critical part of maturation.

The path towards being self-disciplined can begin in school. Early on in this journey, the goal is for the adults to teach responsibility. Having responsibility is an early, but necessary, stage. It is not the same as being self-disciplined.

Adults should begin by letting students set their own goals or create their own situations and then holding kids accountable for following through with their own plans. A few examples of this are: selecting their classes and extracurricular activities, deciding how they spend unstructured time, choosing how they would like to study a topic (such as by picking an assignment or designing an independent study project), and finding ways to improve the school, the community, or the world at large.

Adults have an obligation to aid young people in the thought process needed to make a decision, the appropriate way to judge success or failure, and how to respond to those results. One way that adults can be active in this process by illuminating possibilities and realities that the student perhaps did not see themselves.

But, revealing options does not mean that adults should force students to choose from that list. Part of empowering young people with responsibility requires that students are permitted to make real choices. A real choice is where an individual has the freedom to create their own options; a false choice is a selection amongst only presented options. Illusions do no good—making genuine and independent choices is one of the most empowering experiences in education.

When schools allow students to decide these aspects of their lives they are giving a lot of power to students, and as they grant more power there must be a corresponding rise in student responsibility. Part of helping students be more self-disciplined is to not shield students from the effects of their actions. Young people need to know the effects of their actions, good and bad—it is one of the most valuable lessons an educator can ever teach. This does not mean, however, that adults should abandon kids when, having less experience than adults, they inevitably make a few bad choices.

When a school grants students the power to decide many of their actions and holds them accountable for the results, students will come to see that they—not the adults—are actually in control. The student, then realizing their capacity to produce the results they desire in their lives, must make a significant leap to move from being merely responsible to being self-disciplined. How can a school, having instilled this responsible use of power motivate the student to use the power for the pursuit of self-improvement and self-knowledge? It is a far more difficult challenge than holding students accountable.

The final step on this path is a shift in the student's intent: it is a change to using your free will to improve oneself. Discipline only works to control the actions of others. It does little good in controlling the attitude and motivations of others. This shift cannot be forced through disciplinary measures. The student must choose to do so.

Self-discipline

To create a feeling in the student wherein the student wants to use this power over their lives for the pursuit of self-improvement the school can only suggest and show the student the potential benefits of doing so. It is a case of persuasion and wisdom and not one of force. This means closer student-teacher interaction. Schools must also admit that no matter how well or often done, suasion will not always work. Students can always use this extra power to choose complacency.

When teachers fail to persuade a student, we shouldn't think the individual is lost. People change, and they may not immediately realize that there are benefits to improving one's self and having self-knowledge. It takes time. Not all flowers come into bloom on the first day of spring. Perhaps the student will see the benefits while watching their friends meet the challenge. Perhaps they will be persuaded by another individual during a different time in their life. When, you cannot say, but you can say that it cannot be forced. The job for teachers is to get students to a certain point and then trust them to go the rest of the way.

When a person matures from using their power for pleasing others to using their power to control their actions for self-improvement and self-knowledge, they undergo one of the most meaningful shifts of their life.

EXPERIENTIAL LEARNING

Programs where students apply what they learn in the classroom to an actual situation and also discover new concepts in the process of doing create engaged and inquisitive people. In requiring interaction with the academic content, they compel an immersive learning experience. Jim Barlow helped create such a program—a Model Presidential Nominating Convention for middle and high school students.

Every four years, the Republican and Democratic parties hold presidential nominating conventions to nominate their candidates for president of the United States and approve a political platform for the general election. At these conventions, every state, territory, and the District of Columbia sends delegates to participate in the selection process. For over forty years the Beaverton School District (near Portland, Oregon) organized a model version of this event for student participation and the program educated tens of thousands of young people about the American political system.

It was a realistic convention—complete with boisterous delegates, colorful banners, candidate buttons and noisy bands. Amid all the hoopla, everyone's efforts were directed towards adopting the party's political platform and choosing a nominee. In the months leading up to the event, students delved into every aspect of American economic and social politics. The program taught political subjects and then encouraged the students to apply the knowledge learned in the classroom at the convention.

Students from the participating schools played a number of roles: as members of the candidate and issue caucuses; as delegates to the national platforms, rules, and credentials committees; and as district, state and national chairpersons. The model convention was entirely student run, making it an excellent training tool for student leadership and responsible student behavior. When a school chose to participate, they were given a state to represent and their students researched that state's interests and politics and came to the convention casting votes on all platform and political issues as if they were actually from that state. It culminated in their vote for the convention's nominee for President and Vice President, which again was made from the point-of-view of their state. Each participating school brought as many student delegates to the convention as their state has actual delegates. Therefore, the size of each school's delegation varied depending on the size of the state. For example, if the Democratic Party in the state of Oregon had 56 delegate votes, 56 students will represent the state at the model convention. When an actual state delegation was too large for one school to handle, it was given to two or more schools. Over the last three decades, the convention got so large that the event took over Portland's Memorial Coliseum for four days with 4,000 students attending from all over Oregon and the region.

All permanent committees of the convention met to carry out their business. For instance, there were credentials challenges. Before the convention, students were required to have extensive knowledge about their state to pass a credentialing committee (which is also student-run). This was an example of young people needing to know the facts in order to use them. If the students don't have the background knowledge about their state, the credentialing committee will not allow them to participate. There are platform committees which meet for many months before the convention to draw up a comprehensive policy perspective for the political party for that year. They determined the party's position on every major topic. Discussing complex economic, political and social issues from the perspective of members of the political party requires a tremendous amount of knowledge, and the students immersed themselves and did brilliantly. When these committees presented the platform to the convention, it was opened to all delegates for debate and the engagement with the content continued on the floor of the hall. The convention then began nominations for president and vice president, followed by balloting, which continued for as long as necessary for the convention delegates to reach their choice of who will lead their party. All of these parts in motion created an exciting atmosphere where so much is happening. The student delegates felt the same pressures that delegates feel at the real convention at the model convention.

The model convention became a barometer of the political sentiment in the nation and candidates gained real political power from the event. As a result, model conventions attracted considerable attention from the actual presidential candidates. During the first one in 1964, Nelson Rockefeller visited. At the time his bid for the Republican nomination was floundering, and he was far behind Barry Goldwater. That year the convention was held at a local high school, and the hall was packed full of students. Getting caught up in the enthusiasm of the student delegates, it took Rockefeller thirty minutes to get to the speaker's platform. Weaving his way through a crowd of young people shaking his hand, taking pictures, and shouting his name, Rockefeller began to feel it was a real convention. Rockefeller spoke to hundreds of students, won the model convention nomination, and went on to win the Oregon's real primary—one of his few election victories in 1964. When the dust had settled, the Rockefeller campaign organization credited his appearance at the student convention with playing a vital part in picking up the state of Oregon.

From those relatively humble beginnings, it has gone on to become a prominent fixture in Oregon presidential politics.

Bobby Kennedy, George McGovern, Hubert Humphrey, Scoop Jackson, Frank Church, Jesse Jackson, Harold Stassen, Jimmy Carter, Jerry Brown, Ronald Reagan, George H. W. Bush, Michael Dukakis, and Bill Clinton, along with other candidates, all put in personal appearances and gave speeches to the students. Major candidates also invested staff time and money, and Frank Church and George H. W. Bush brought their real floor leaders from the actual convention to assist the students and try and gain a model convention victory. Governors, Senators, members of the House of Representatives, and mayors have all attended.

It attracted media attention, which helped to make it realistic. Over the years, all of the national networks and local television stations, as well as many cable stations, reported on the conventions, some even brought journalists to broadcast live from the convention floor. Many national and local newspapers and magazines covered it too. Once a reporter from a national news magazine remarked that it was "more real than the real convention." That may be philosophically impossible, but it illustrates the authenticity of this event.

This type of program was successful because it took into account the great diversity of our students. Some students excel at research; some are better at small group discussions; others like speaking assignments; while others prefer leadership roles. There were opportunities for secretarial work, radio and television reporting, speech writing and creating art. This program needed all of these, and there was a job for everyone; and through it all, everyone learned about politics.

In an atmosphere of genuine struggle, the convention generated an understanding of and an interest in the American political system that stayed with the students long after they have left high school. Most of them had so much fun they didn't realize they had learned anything until they went home.

This was a case in which students applied what they were studying in the classroom to real-life or realistic situations and learned new ideas in the process of doing something authentic. The nominating convention is but one option that could be implemented. Another possible program could be an environmental policy convention to remake America and the world. Many options are available and can occur in every discipline. They just need realization.

ADMINISTRATION

The primary objective of every school's administration is to serve the needs of the staff and students.

The first step may be creating the right tone. Schools are these hives of human activity with hundreds of people across the entire spectrum of age, from kids just starting out to older teachers nearing retirement. Without the right atmosphere, the school can become a highly fractured and stressful place where the paths of communication and action are unclear, and the adults find themselves fearing the intentions of others and divesting themselves from the school. In the best atmosphere, a feeling develops between everyone, like a grand dance it becomes a place of movement, growth, and joy. Successful administrators can do a number of things to establish an environment where students and staff work together and love spending their time.

It all begins with openness, for transparency leads to honesty, and these two together lead to trust. Creating an environment of trust should be an objective of administrative bodies everywhere, and especially those in schools. Administrators should start with themselves and act as a model of what they would like to see: transparency and regular frank dialogue. When everyone in the school—adults and students—can speak freely, there will be more opportunities to make suggestions and for good ideas to be heard. Moreover, this can reduce the suspicion, fear, and rumors that often arise in large bureaucracies all while increasing collaboration. Teachers need to hear administrators and administrators need to hear teachers, and both need to listen to their students.

It seems to be the case that when there is openness, honesty, and trust, that mutual respect and ownership often follow. Administrators can foster this by enabling everyone to be involved in decisions affecting their department and encouraging creativity on the part of all teachers and support staff, including the maintenance and cafeteria persons, and the kids. Staff committees and student groups can be the creative force behind new and powerful ways to improve the school. Such a process is very empowering. Empowering everyone also involves deferring to their ideas and trusting their professional opinions. With collaboration and openness being major objectives, the school can become a real community where, in this atmosphere of mutual respect, both teachers and students develop a real sense of ownership.

When all of this is in place, it becomes natural for everyone to experience the joy of putting in the work to be a part of the school; everyone's shared goal is to improve. At this point, there is an atmosphere of unfettered movement and optimism. In addition to creating an environment where others can fulfill their potential, administrators can also serve their school through their own merits.

Great administrators are people of action, doing what is necessary to improve the school so teachers can best improve students' lives. For example, they can take charge of discipline cases that teachers cannot handle alone and help to establish a school-wide code of conduct. They can be responsible for contact with the community, understanding that good communication about the school will motivate parents and neighborhood groups and programs to be part of the school community. And in listening to many sources, they can make thoughtful decisions and create paths for success. Further, these administrators provide technical support for the teaching staff, and they are a central part of the evaluation process for teachers and staff.

The most effective administrators are facilitators of trust, open communication, and mutual respect, and are people of action. Nothing prevents every administrator and every administration from being so.

TEACHER EVALUATION AND TENURE

The goal for everyone—administrators, teachers, students, and parents—is for their school to be full of wonderful and capable teachers. While it's difficult to conceptualize a definition of a "good teacher" that would apply to every educator, the critical process of evaluation should involve many perspectives and cannot be boiled down to holding particular certificates or having certain years of experience or be based upon a few short classroom visits by an administrator. We need a better formula for professional assessment and administrators should seek out and listen to the opinions of many people: evaluators, teachers, parents, and especially, students.

At present, teacher evaluation is usually conducted by a small handful of individuals, generally former teachers who are current administrators. Their opinion is an excellent one to have, but their interaction with the teacher can be better. Professional evaluators often spend their time explaining their teaching philosophy and then expect the teacher to adopt that philosophy. That is an unhelpful model for appraisal. Sometimes when a new method in teaching comes around, these evaluators like the sound of it and insist that all the teachers use it. Creators of new styles and techniques recognize that they can be applied effectively by some and not so effectively by others. Success with a method depends on the individual educator, their personality, and their students. Some administrators insist that all teachers exclusively use one technique and their performance is judged on how well they do it. If the new method—or any method for that matter—does not fit the teacher and they are still expected to use it, the teacher suffers, the students suffer, and the school in general suffers. Administrators should adopt the rule that if the strategy fits, use it. If it doesn't fit, don't use it—but never insist that all teachers use the same system. Teachers should have the freedom to abandon what ceases to be useful.

Other times these evaluators remain stolidly focused on the teaching methods used during their years in the classroom. Although the old approaches may still seem logical, the students to whom the methods must apply have changed. Continued contact is crucial because students change and as they do, so should teaching techniques. Good teachers change with them. If you are not in the classroom, adapting is very difficult. This is not an indictment of the evaluator; rather, it is the reality of this situation.

Then there are those administrators who judge teachers on whether or not they run an orderly classroom and keep strict discipline. Creativity does not always fit into that model. One teacher in our acquaintance ran a rather loose classroom and did not insist that the students sit in straight rows. She was a very good, very creative and loving teacher. On one particular day the students were at work in groups. It was very educational productive controlled chaos. Her evaluator came by the classroom, stood in the doorway, glanced about and spoke to this first-year teacher in a voice that could be heard for a hundred feet, "What do you call this, a classroom for learning or playtime?" The class came to a screeching halt. The students quieted down, and the teacher broke into tears. The evaluator then walked down the hall. This is a perfect example of an ineffective and closed-minded evaluator.

A skilled evaluator is a good listener, and good evaluation is the product of open communication. The conversation would be best if it began by the teacher explaining his or her teaching philosophy. This is good for three reasons. First, it allows the teacher to share their professional beliefs and experiences and permits the evaluator to attempt to see the classroom from the perspective of the teacher. Second, the evaluator can give their opinion as to whether or not the teacher is following and succeeding in their own philosophy. Third, the teacher might well hear good suggestions of other things that might be worthwhile in the classroom. As the discussion continues the administrator can describe their perspective of what they saw when they visited. Not only narrating what the class looked like from where they sat, but they can also offer meaningful compliments, suggestions, and concerns. Everyone can benefit from another viewpoint. Again, this should occur not as a lecture from a supervisor, but within the framework of a conversation between two professionals.

In addition to this evaluator's perspective, regular time should be set aside for peer assessment based upon classroom visits from numerous colleagues from the same building. Having educators watch their colleagues teach provides the administration another expert opinion about the assessed teacher, and also allows the observing teachers professional development by watching different methods and styles. The beauty of this system is that it benefits the observed teacher and the observing teachers. It also chips away at the isolation many teachers feel and improves opportunities for collaboration. After multiple observations, these colleagues then give their feedback to the administrative team and the observed teacher.

Teachers also know how other teachers behave professionally because they work in close proximity, discussing teaching techniques and the content of courses with each other. Some of the best teaching evaluation comes from insight received from these conversations. While forward-facing teachers always look for ways to improve, and self-examinations through informal peer dialogue are always fruitful, it's necessary to require these visits and conversations.

Professional and peer evaluation will not provide a full picture to administrators, and other opinions should be sought. Students and parents should also be encouraged to comment on teachers, and while they must not be the final say in a teacher's employment status, the administration should seek out and listen to their concerns with the same patience and interest they afford teachers and evaluators.

Students are the people who know best about what goes on in the classroom day in and day out, and as a great direct source of information they should also be a part of the evaluation process. In addition to telling the teacher on a regular informal basis what worked, they can write a short evaluation in the middle and the end of the semester saying what they liked about class or a teacher, discuss what they are learning, and which specific methods and topics were successful, as well as any concerns they may have. One copy could go to the teacher and the other to the administration. Many teachers view this as too threatening and believe that their employment will be tied to being merely popular. But this process isn't intended to be intimidating. What their students are giving is their opinion, and it can be very helpful to improve their ability to learn and the teacher's ability to teach. And with the administration receiving views from multiple perspectives, a popular but ineffective teacher will be found out.

Parents can provide a different type of feedback. As community members, individual parents should not be able to dictate who is hired or fired and what material is covered in classes, but they should be involved in the process of giving the administrators additional perspectives.

The formal assessment process can be non-threatening and used to improve not intimidate. The process should be an enjoyable exercise in which the teacher appreciates the exchange of ideas with all involved, especially the students. All these sources ought to provide the teacher and administration enough feedback for continued improvement to take place. Teachers are like medical doctors in that the practice of education is just that, it is a practice. There is never an end point. As the practice continues, the practitioners must change as the world, and the people in it, change. To remain static is to fall behind, and in many cases, never to catch up again. A forward-facing and positive teacher continually evaluates their methods, and as a result adjusts to match the needs of their students.

In the end, after an administration receives these many perspectives, it may be the case that a particular teacher cannot be improved or that there are concerns about a teacher's effectiveness and it is determined that they should be let go. When there is a need to fire bad teachers, there must be a mechanism. Some schools maintain a system of tenure or an arrangement like it that ensures that most teachers, good and bad, may keep their jobs regardless of how effective they are in the classroom. Tenure-provided job security would be great if all employees were excellent; however, that is almost never the case. Many outstanding teachers embrace tenure, acknowledging that while it can harbor weak educators, it also allows them to lead an open classroom without micromanagement or fear of reprisal. This is no way to improve the lives of young people. We have to have great teachers, and we can't have a system that automatically retains people merely because they are alive and were hired in the first place.

Experience is no guarantee of competence. We have both bore witness to those who spent decades in front of a classroom yet still have no business being with young people. And pleasantly, we have seen many examples of educators brilliantly doing a great job early in their careers. There are those who improve over time and those who get complacent, bored, and ineffective in a few short years. Teaching must be dynamic and school should not be a place where one could gain such firm job security that one could hole-up for the rest of their careers and avoid working. Teachers should never lose their jobs for merely political reasons. There were many cases back in the 1950s and 1960s where teachers were fired because of politics, such as discussing communism, Vietnam, or social upheaval.

In the early sixties, Jim Barlow was teaching lessons on political and economic theory where he compared various types of government and economic systems, such as socialism, communism, and capitalism, as well as democratic and authoritarian systems. Many in the suburban community felt that teaching the concept of communism in relation to other systems had no place in the school. Parents discussed what they should do. They wanted to fire him. Although Jim didn't know it at the time, controversy was brewing for a number of weeks. It culminated with a massive meeting of about three hundred people in the school cafeteria. Typically only a dozen or so came to these meetings. Jim was asked to attend but had no idea what the meeting was about or why he needed to be there.

In full view of the assembled parents, Jim was seated across a table from the chairman of the local Parent Teacher Association. The head of the PTA told Jim that they thought he was a communist and so would like to see him fired. Jim responded by saying that he would like to ask the chair some questions. Jim asked the chairman if he would like him to teach about the American political system. He answered, "Well, sure." Jim went on to ask if capitalism should be taught. He answered, "Yes, that would be appropriate." Jim replied by saying that most students don't know anything about other political and economic systems and asked if it would be ok for them to know about it so they can make a comparison. If the American system is good, then does the chair think that students should be able to make comparisons between our system and others? The chairman agreed. Jim asked if that also applied to learning about Cuba, China, and Western European countries, because how can you make a judgment if you only knew one side of the story. There were murmurs from the parents. The chairman thought for a while, and then asked, "So, is that what you do?"

The will of those assembled in that cafeteria was such that they really didn't want variety and only wanted one position taught, but there were some parents there of an opposite position. Looking back, maybe it was a bit of luck, but as a result of that minority voice in the crowd, the chair reluctantly agreed that variety was the best course of action and said that he understood the teacher's point of view. The meeting broke up as cooler heads prevailed, and Jim was permitted to continue teaching. He did, however, have the reputation of being a communist for the next 40 years. That event did not lead to Jim's termination, but there are other cases in smaller districts where teachers were let go for similar reasons.

Evolution, war, immigration, religion, politics, sexuality, and social and racial class issues are some topics that also get teachers into trouble. Teachers ought to be able to discuss multiple perspectives and unpopular positions to controversial issues, and they should be able to do so without fear of losing their jobs.

A structure replacing tenure would be best if it had four parts in place: one, the promotion of open minds and open communication within the teaching ranks as well as with students, parents, and administrators; two, educators judged on subject knowledge and instructional skill, not length of employment; three, the ability for the administration to act on information about teachers; and four, a strong protection for academic liberty in the classroom. It's possible to have a structure that permits unfettered academic freedom yet also serves as a watchdog assuring only the best are on staff, the mediocre are improved, and the bad are let go.

Teaching is a sacred profession. Special care must be taken to ensure that young people are in the best hands.

TEACHER COLLABORATIONS

No matter one's experience or expertise, one can always benefit from the visions and strengths of others. The strongest teachers collaborate for the same reason as students: as an active acknowledgment that other people can assist in finding solutions to shared and individual goals.

There are many advantages for educators who develop a culture of collaboration. For one, by engaging in peer criticism and trading ideas about teaching styles and their students' learning styles, the craft of every teacher improves. Moreover, educators who work together can often create more interesting projects, classes, and extracurricular activities than they could on their own. This not only applies to a department but also across departments and schools. And lastly, in our experience, collaboration is vital for finding joy in daily life, strengthening social bonds and developing respect for others and empathy.

Schools have the opportunity to mitigate some of the problems of students who might have a disjointed home life, however in order for the student-teacher relationship to advance to the point where teachers can do so effectively, teachers and educators need to work together and make each other aware of what the other is doing and act as a mutual support system. Teachers need to share what they know about students who are in distress or seem to be having troubles at home. In a society where family bonds are weakening and as schools attempt to fill a major place in the community, educators must be there for each other as a strong positive interconnected force.

This process requires communication. Although this may seem obvious, it's not a case of collaboration following communication like summer following spring, but rather, more like the relationship between the chicken and the egg. Action and discussion require the other for either to succeed. Teachers easily fall into circumstances where they teach their classes, grade their papers, do their work, and after a full and tiring day, go home. Getting the opportunity to sit and have a meaningful conversation with their peers often lies in want. Time should be set aside for this—a lot of it. Now, meetings have accumulated a bit of a stigma as a euphemism for a collection of people wasting their time together, but they needn't be so. They shouldn't be a repetitive exercise of restating buzz words and action-free calls for encouragement. Meetings must have a purpose.

There can be different styles of meetings with different purposes and different member compositions. There is no need for every employee to come to every meeting the school holds or to be involved in every matter afoot on campus. Some meetings can be about content (and attended by members of that department), others can be about new teacher training (composed of novices and some veterans), and some can be divided into projects or program groups (such as an extracurricular activity or school-wide technology). Some meetings would be to teach each other, some to compare academic material, and others to discuss the specific needs of a shared group of students. And just as great collaboration cannot occur without an open line of near constant communication, so too can discussions feel pointless unless there are applications for it.

Schools don't need to descend into a labyrinth of subcommittees where much is discussed but little time is left to do anything. There can be a balance. A meeting shouldn't be a paper tiger unable to do anything without constant approval, where the administrative body micromanages the work of a group of teachers. There must be a willingness to delegate and let tasks be completed by those so empowered. If an administration wants teachers to buy into spending their time collaborating in meetings, they need to step back and allow those meetings to develop their own ideas and directions.

New teachers have much to gain from increased peer communication. An excellent way to learn is through a setup similar to the old apprentice system referred to today as mentoring. A mentor—be it one teacher or a group of teachers—can be of great benefit in aiding a novice's way through the daily grind of entering a new profession. This is commonplace in many jobs, be they law firms, hospitals, or artisans, why not also schools? Why is education a profession where after getting hired an individual is so often handed their full duties and expected to figure it out? With a set up like that can there be any surprise when so many young teachers leave the profession in their first few years? A mentor can act as a sounding board for new ideas and daily frustrations. They can discuss teaching philosophies and offer suggestions on how to improve. They can help begin parent-teacher relationships and show ways through the inevitable heaps of paperwork.

But just as it's no good that new teachers quit in high numbers and that the structure compels them to either sink or swim, it's also no good to force or assign a mentor teacher. The real solution is in creating a community where teachers choose to work together and are encouraged to collaborate. The real solution is teachers becoming friends. The administration can move this process forward by respecting teacher initiatives, allowing teachers to create ownership over their projects and ideas, and publically acknowledging and rewarding teamwork when it happens.

Administrators also should push teachers to be in situations that encourage future collaboration. For example, it would also be very meaningful for educators to see how other classes are taught. Teachers could watch their peers in their department, as well as those across departments and age levels. And it need not be restricted to new teachers—everyone can learn from each other—even the veterans from the rookies. There is no need to assume that the younger ones have less to offer their peers than the teachers with decades of experience. The young can energize the old and act as a reminder about the reasons they entered this profession so many years before, and they could also expose their elders to new information and demonstrate new teaching styles and technologies. And having sat in on each other's class, they will be more likely to chat during passing times and work together after the last bell rings. We understand that having substitutes cover classes on occasion so teachers could be paid to watch their peers costs money. Paying teachers to not teach might sound ridiculous—but it's not. Teachers also need to be learners, seeing for themselves other options and new ways of teaching. Everyone benefits when the school becomes a place where friends work together.

Educators need not become mad scientists, working long hours in solitude, immersed within their pet projects and lessons. In all walks of academia, great things happen when teachers and intellectuals work together. One of the reasons why our country produces so many Nobel Prize winners is our universities have a culture of cooperative work—not only within a campus but across campuses. The overwhelming majority of recent prizes in chemistry, physics, and medicine are shared. Great things can happen when we come together to help each other.

CULTURE

Formal education can provide an insight into our way of life beyond what can be gained at home or in the streets. Schools may be the first place where young people have the opportunity to learn about democracy, literature, religion, art, and others aspects of our culture in a meaningful way. It is important to teach our young people what our culture is, some reasons why it is, and its role in the world. One of the great, often under-acknowledged, purposes of schools is the teaching of our culture.

American culture is also taught indirectly through interactions in class and in the hallways, during extracurricular activities, and through collaborations and conversations with people different than one's family. In this way teaching culture is more than making young people aware of our history, it is an active participation in our culture through social interaction. Schools have great power to shape American culture and society.

Schools can be places where we seek justifications for why our society is what it is. It can be easy to internalize one's culture and view it as natural and not reflect on our way of life, however, educators should not shy away from inspecting our values, our social norms, and our institutions. Students should engage everything from gender roles to laws, from our relationship with the environment to consumerism.

Educators can show why previous generations molded our lifestyle into what it is and compel young people to ask themselves if those reasons are outmoded for their world. Students should see themselves as a part of the creation of their society, asking themselves if they wish to perpetuate it or if they wish to change it in some way. Culture is transmitted from one generation to the next, but never without modifications. It is organic; always in motion. Through new experiences, young people can change our culture. They will live longer than us and will surely shape the American culture that exists today into a form that is meaningful to their world, a world that is beginning to exist in their minds. Every generation takes this task upon itself, and the best we can do is plant a seed. Theirs is a most important task, for the shape of American culture is of great significance in the twenty-first century.

In the modern world, our culture spreads the furthest. It exists across the globe, from once remote regions to cultures that dislike our government's policies. The type of government we fashioned and the economic structure we molded are now the dominate forms across the planet. Our music, our food, our movies are everywhere. While often modified and appropriated to be relevant and accessible in their new home, there is no doubt that some of its roots can be found here, in our country. The language of the world's cultures has an increasingly American accent. With globalization, it seems clear that our nation's very palpable export is our culture. Young Americans should be aware of this. They can be active in its creation. It must be what they want it to be.

Equally important is for our youth to know the world beyond our shores. Teachers can illuminate the planet's many cultures—rich in their own social structures, histories and unique ways of problem-solving. They can learn about other ways of life, other religions, other traditions, other philosophies, other struggles, other achievements, and prides.

An education in the diversity of cultures instills understanding, develops empathy, reduces fear, and increases self-reflection.

PREPARING FOR THE WORKFORCE

No matter if it is a technical school or a broad liberal arts school, the best way formal education can prepare young people for the workforce is by focusing on engendering a warm heart and a keen mind. Careers are often remade many times in a lifetime; schools can help young people be flexible in their future career choices.

Creativity. Curiosity. Critical thinking. Problem solving. Decision making. Honesty. Responsibility. Self-discipline. Self-knowledge. Cooperation. Empathy. Listening to others. An open mind. Working with the knowledge base you have. All jobs need these; all individuals would benefit from having them.

DROPPING OUT

Too many students are being pushed out of formal education because of the choices schools make. While it is true that some are pulled away by complex societal and economic motivations (such as family and employment pressures), this is an area in which individual educators don't have so much immediate control over. Teachers and administrators will find it more fruitful to take the time to reflect on and question aspects of which they do have control.

The list of reasons why a young person might leave prior to matriculation is long and the prospective dropout, their classmates, teachers and administrators might well disagree as to the causes. Those who choose to drop out do so after making a complex decision based on their belief of the diploma's worth compared to the time and effort to receive one in the traditional manner. Students may leave because the school system does not teach relevant matters. Some students walk away after frustrations with an immobile system whose rejoinder to their requests is, "This is the way it is. Take it or leave it." Others' choice is in response to an infrastructure that focuses its energy on the college-bound, dismissing less academic future careers as irrelevant. And others do so after boredom with mindless busywork or defeat at the jaws of a bureaucratic beast. Some go because their teachers imply that they will never succeed, and some because their schoolmates say the same. Potential drop-outs see others' success (and their lack of it) as having taken on a pattern. They may feel that tracking, standardized testing, and disciplinary programs only reinforce their lack. These are real concerns. They are stigmatized and may feel that there is no hope.

Many drop out not realizing the long-term implications of the decision. It is up to adults, those with greater experience, to convince young people not to leave school. The standard approach tries to stem the dropout rate through academic programs. Some allow students more time with teachers. Others aim at re-teaching fundamentals. All of these can do a great deal of good. However, remedial education must exercise extreme caution and not mutate into detention. It will not be effective if there is no attempt to aid the students in improving their whole self—a self beyond academics.

If schools want students to come to school, we need to make students have a feeling of belonging and purpose. There should be a focus on creating positive attachments to the space. A school garden is an example of a program that could be established to improve a student's relationship with their school. By working in the garden, the young person has a medium to interact with the school beyond doing homework and taking tests—they contribute to their school's aesthetic value and make it a pleasant place they care about. They might take pride in the flowers that bloom or vegetables that grow—nurturing a sense of purpose, responsibility, and accomplishment. All the while, a connection between them, their school and their fellow gardening schoolmates begins to blossom. When young people start to feel that they are needed for something meaningful at school, they are not only less likely to drop out, but they will also be more likely to come to school regularly. Many extracurricular activities succeed in this task of bringing young people to school and allowing them to enrich themselves through caring for other people and their school.

Another intangible factor in the dropout rate is perception: perception of the self and the educational system's perception of the student. To reduce the number of young people dropping out, there is a need to transform the students' negative self-image and their low opinion both of school and of themselves as students. There is also a need to modify the teachers' and fellow students' perception that these young people are lost causes. These are the major challenges in repairing the minds of students and teachers alike.

One final item worth serious consideration is that we believe everyone should have the freedom to abandon what ceases to be useful. This implies that young people should have the ability to leave school if it fails to meet their needs as learners. After all, there is not only one right way to get an education. In some cases, the best decision is to leave high school before graduation. For some, their energy may be best spent elsewhere. Adults should encourage students to think about their lives and understand that life is a series of choices—and in turn, that many options are open: including leaving school. If some, so empowered, elect to drop out, what should they be "dropping into"? We shouldn't feel that we are encouraging students to drop out when we build options for those that do. America needs more alternatives, be they trade schools, apprenticeships, or collectives. There needs to be civil service organizations where a young person could constructively spend a year or two and later return to high school if the time was right.

The most optimistic belief anyone can hold is that there are always choices. Students should know that there is a choice to drop out. The task for educators is to urge students that the best option for their present life and their future may be to stay in school. And the best way for schools to be persuasive is by adjusting aspects of school structure so that every student feels a sense of importance and belonging and has the opportunity to learn.

COMMUNITY

School populations can be a living society: integrated with their neighborhood and be a positive reflection of that outside community. Schools that choose to interact with the whole community encourage their students to be involved with the people and organizations that make up their community.

One high school that comes to mind had a class on childcare, and within the school there was a daycare center with children on the premises and often throughout the halls. That same school had a class of students with developmental disabilities who had access to the entire building. The mainstream students often helped out, and some of these students attended mainstream classes. The result was that the mainstream students developed an understanding of people with certain limitations and the students with disabilities enjoyed being with the general student body and expanded their education. These two programs greatly benefited all the students and gave them a greater understanding of the total community in which they lived. On top of these programs, the building was used for weekly meetings of several community groups, which added another dimension to the school. Occasionally one of these groups, a retired people's organization, had the school's culinary classes prepare lunch for their meetings.

As diversity continues to be a pursuit of modern policymakers, the obvious seems to be forgotten: diversity exists throughout every community. It exists when groups of different people interact positively together. What better way to demonstrate diversity than to bring the diverse elements of a community into schools? Showing young people the many options in life—and the differences within society and humanity—ought to be one of the purposes of school. We can do this by encouraging young people to grow up alongside a wide sweep of their own community. When students do so they will not only learn about the lives of others, but they will be confident to see themselves as a part of society today—not simply as 'future citizens'. They can interact with—and if need be, change—the community they live in now.

In some neighborhoods the community lacks cooperative cohesion. It needs help. Schools can bring light to the community and be a source of strength. They should never shy away from the positive power they have.

A school such as that is a great place to be. Everyone would benefit: the students, the faculty, the groups that use the school, and the neighbors. School becomes more relevant because it adopts the community as a whole. All schools should make the time and effort to include their communities and create a diverse mix of groups that can all interact together. Everyone would benefit.

WHY TEACH?

So why get into this profession? What brings people into teaching? It doesn't seem to be the money or the glamor. From the educators we've known, the best do it for the love of it. It sounds corny, but it's true.

The inspirational ones invest themselves in their classroom because they love their students and their academic subject. Their passion casts a glow about them. These adults help students bring forth a love of learning and bring young people to the point where they have confidence in themselves as intellectuals. This includes helping students to know how to seek information, how to apply that knowledge, think critically and creatively, and gain wisdom through its application. They also help students be in a position to gain self-knowledge and self-discipline and encourage cooperation and the creation of new experience. Great educators desire young people confident in themselves as human beings, unintimidated by the world beyond.

The finest also choose this career because of their love for their community. This profession grants the opportunity to help young people become active in their neighborhood and develop a concern for one another. Civics is not a matter restricted to a few weeks of social studies classes. Not only do these educators teach students to care about their society, but the best also live their lessons and stay involved in the community in which they live and work. The compassionate ones who enter this profession realize that since they work closely with young people and know the issues facing them, they have a responsibility to advocate on behalf of children. They are teachers because they want to be involved in the present community and want to shape how it will be in the future.

Every day in the classroom is a day interacting in the public eye. In the act of teaching the growth-oriented and self-reflective ones reassess their understanding of the material, and through their students are continually exposed to new ideas, perspectives, and challenges. By being an educator, they are engaging in an act that forces them to always learn and gain greater self-knowledge. While many professionals are stuck in careers with monotonous repetition and a lack of challenges, teaching provides a distinct counterpoint.

The finest become teachers out of love for their students and themselves, their community and the future.

In fact, it's just fun.

CONCLUSION

PURPOSE OF SCHOOLS

A school is a special place.

Institutions of education have a greater opportunity to improve the lives of young people and benefit future generations than any other public service. Schools can help young people to know themselves so that they can engage in their life and the world around them in an enthusiastic and unfettered way.

As one of the most pervasive and active public institutions in our neighborhoods, schools can improve the greater community, be part of the greater community, and provide a loving community for students. Schools have tremendous potential to mitigate social problems. One of the purposes of schools is to be an actively beneficial force in the neighborhood as a fear-free and positive community center. And just as schools have the potential to improve the community they are in, they also have the responsibility to provide a good environment for children while class is in session. It must be somewhere that all young people—regardless of academic success—can grow and cultivate connections in a positive atmosphere removed of fear.

In this setting, young people can learn about the world and our relationship with it. Education is not only names, dates, and formulas. School is a social entity and so can be more than a place to read books and to take tests. It can be a place of interactive involvement with academic materials, where young people are pushed and challenged. Here adults can promote creativity and actively teach students to think critically. Here students learn about the world by engaging in it. Young people are urged to examine multiple perspectives, issues in greater depth, and areas of study which they may not seek out themselves. And more than all of that, schools can foster a joyful love of learning.

Schools can also be a vehicle to teach the younger generation our culture and give students a broad worldview by teaching them about other societies. Educators have an obligation to ask American young people to consider the values of our very powerful and widespread culture. In the classroom and in the hallways, students can to be shown how they affect the world around them and how to take an active role in the human experience. Through a broad curriculum we can help young people become members of a perceptive and involved public, prepared for their life outside of school, both at present and after graduation.

One of the best ways young people can be ready is to leave the schoolhouse door with the desire and capability to create new positive experiences in the world. This can be done by promoting collaboration and the ability and desire to work with other people. Schools can engender empathic hearts, along with keen minds and active citizens. Young people can have opportunities to create their own situations and challenges and then be held accountable for their actions. In doing so, schools assist young people onto a path toward having self-discipline and self-knowledge. Students need to be shown the options they have in life. They ought to be urged to try new things and experiment to see what they like and what they are good at—what are today's clubs and science projects, might well someday be their career.

We shouldn't forget that from when a person is six until they are eighteen, they will spend more hours in school and doing school-related activities than they will doing anything else. For twelve impressionable years their lives turn on it. Educators should appreciate the power they possess to affect their students. By teaching content using the methods and attitudes we mention in the book, educators can help create young people ready to live fully. Administrators and teachers, board members and politicians, must all be conscious of the great many things schools can be and the great number of benefits it can bring to present and future generations.

Our American institution has many purposes, but its supreme purpose is as a place of hope—hope for the future and hope for making our society what it can be.

ACKNOWLEDGMENTS

This book is the result of many years of conversations. As such, there have been many people who offered their input, and this book wouldn't be the same without them. We would like to thank our families. Additionally, we would like to thank those who read the manuscript and provided feedback and in particular Tim Foster, Emilee Naik, and Ashley-Jayne Nicolaus. Emily Aslin at Honeybones Design designed the cover.

ABOUT THE AUTHORS

James Barlow taught high school social studies courses for over 40 years in the Beaverton, Oregon from 1962 to 2005. During his long career as an educator, he was the recipient of numerous local and national awards for his teaching. Jim also held senior leadership roles within Oregon High School International Relations League Model United Nations, the Oregon Council for the Social Studies, and Advanced Placement Teachers of the State of Oregon. In 1964 he founded the Model Presidential Nominating Convention and led it for four decades. Conventions brought together thousands of students from across the region in a boisterous and authentic multi-day simulation run entirely by high school students. It became an important fixture in Oregon presidential politics and grew so large that it was held at the Memorial Coliseum for the last three decades. National leaders such as Nelson Rockefeller, Robert Kennedy, George McGovern, Hubert Humphrey, Jesse Jackson, Jimmy Carter, Ronald Reagan, George H.W. Bush, Michael Dukakis, and Bill Clinton, amongst many others, visited and gave speeches to high school students. A life-long Portland, Oregon resident and a descendent of a famous Oregon Trail pioneer, Jim lives with his wife and cats.

Anil Naik was a high school student under James Barlow. He has traveled to 50 countries across the Middle East, Asia, Africa, and Europe, including teaching in an International Baccalaureate World School in Beirut, Lebanon. He continues to be actively involved with the International Baccalaureate. His interests are in anthropology and world history. A son of Indian immigrants, he currently teaches high school social studies courses in Beaverton, Oregon, where he lives with his wife and two young boys.

Made in the USA
Monee, IL
07 January 2022

88279653R20073